HOPE
FOR MAN

*An Optimistic Philosophy
and
Guide to Self-Fulfillment*

BY

Joshua Loth Liebman

A Sequel to "Peace of Mind"

SIMON AND SCHUSTER

NEW YORK

SECOND PRINTING

LIBRARY OF CONGRESS CATALOG CARD NUMBER: 66-13846
MANUFACTURED IN THE UNITED STATES OF AMERICA
BY H. WOLFF BOOK MFG. CO., NEW YORK
DESIGNED BY EDITH FOWLER

Preface

Joshua Loth Liebman, author of the famous book *Peace of Mind*, was a multifaceted human being; intellectually demanding of himself to an unbelievable degree, a perfectionist, compassionate, yet "filled with," as he himself wrote at the age of twenty-four, "a consuming fire to bring forth from the immortals of the ages glowing coals with which to sear the minds and hearts of the American community." Out of his feeling of great debt to depth psychology and his empathy with the emotionally suffering men and women in our age, he wrote *Peace of Mind* to point out the universality of certain basic human problems and some of the methods for seeking help in resolving them.

I believe that my late husband's book brought understanding and with it genuine peace of mind to a large proportion of those literally millions of men and women who read the book. He was barely forty-one when he died unexpectedly, and his book had been out only two years. But the fact that he inspired and comforted millions is attested to in the citation accompanying the posthumous award of an honorary degree of Doctor of Letters from Colby College. It read in part: "Minister not only to your congregation at Temple Israel but through your books and radio

5

lectures to a large and ever-growing audience, you have helped to bridge not only the chasms between faiths but the rifts within the human soul and have aided your countrymen in achieving that most cherished of possessions—peace of mind." To render that aid, I know, was what he most wanted when he wrote the book.

But the publication of that book, completed when he was not yet forty, had many other results, and I should like, in introducing this new book, *Hope for Man,* to speak briefly of two of them.

One, now perhaps too infrequently remembered, is the great impetus that *Peace of Mind* gave to pastoral psychiatry, the encouragement it gave to the development of the now wide movement of practical and spiritual aid to countless thousands through clinics, through churches of many denominations, and through many publications by the use of the combined insights of religion and of modern psychiatry. That, indeed, is the theme running through *Peace of Mind,* and it is reasonable to assume that many of the fine programs for helping the psychologically and morally perplexed developed since the publication of the book received their initial inspiration from it.

The other result I should like to mention is a somewhat more personal one, as it is also partially, but only partially, the reason I wished to have the present book published. The fact is that *Peace of Mind* is so heavily oriented—and quite properly so, of course—toward modern psychiatry that many have thought that, outside of religion, Dr. Liebman's entire interest lay in psychology. Psychology was, of course, one of his major interests—but only one. He earned his doctor's degree, as a matter of fact, in philosophy, his first love; he was deep-read in many fields of literature; he had more than a casual interest in music and art;

he was no mere tyro in physics and mathematics; and he was always well versed in politics and national and international affairs. Among his friends he numbered scientists and senators, artists and novelists, university presidents, Nobel Prize winners and, of course, many spiritual leaders of all faiths.

With his inquiring mind, before his first book was published, he was laying the cornerstone of a second book, which he entitled *Hope for Man*. Years ahead of his time, he saw the dangers of the teachings of the new pessimists, their nihilism, which he hoped to refute with his own philosophy of life. Its theme clearly was to be an answer to the pessimism in much of modern literature and philosophy, particularly existentialism as set forth in Kierkegaard and Sartre, as well as the brilliant but narrow view of life represented in such dark writers as Kafka. These were among the subjects on which he had frequently lectured, preached, and spoken informally, especially with me.

Many people, including our daughter, Dr. Leila Liebman, and Dr. Lydia G. Dawes, knowing of the plans for a second book, urged me to gather materials together and publish them. I refused. In fact, I did not feel even like looking through the literally hundreds of pounds of manuscript lectures, essays and sermons placed in files in a Boston warehouse. Human memory and *Peace of Mind* were, I thought, sufficient monument to any man.

But years later I received a suggestion from one of Dr. Liebman's closest friends and mine, Leon Shimkin. Mr. Shimkin is an exact coeval of my husband's—that is, they were born on the same day and in the same year. "Birthday brothers" they used to call themselves. Mr. Shimkin, a partner in the firm of Simon and Schuster, made his suggestion with the enthusiastic endorsement of his co-partner, M. Lincoln Schuster, whom my husband

and I also claimed as a dear friend. Knowing of my husband's project, Mr. Shimkin suggested, over two years ago, that now I should work through those manuscripts to see whether I might be able to reconstruct the book my husband had had in mind and which he had discussed so often with me. I frankly felt both unwilling and unable to make such an effort; yet my friend was insistent that some attempt should be made.

When I realized Mr. Shimkin was correct, I recognized that my position as a full-time psychiatric social worker would prevent my giving adequate time to this great endeavor. After serious consideration I chose Selma Weiss Stone, a trusted friend of Dr. Liebman's and mine, to be the literary assistant, with Mr. Shimkin's complete approval. She was engaged to research all of Dr. Liebman's works. Soon I was giving every spare moment to the arduous work on the project, and finally we received very valuable help from both Mr. Shimkin and from some of the editorial staff of Simon and Schuster. Among the papers Mrs. Stone dramatically came upon was the outline for *Hope for Man,* which enabled us to prepare this manuscript for publication.

What has emerged is not a book that follows exactly the original rough outline of an answer to some modern pessimists, though there is plenty of that, too, as we found when the files were open. It is really a much broader book, though the basic theme is the same. It is broader because it does not merely answer negativism; it is a positive statement of a modern, practical, and basically very optimistic philosophy, one that embraces life instead of rejecting it. In it one will find again Dr. Liebman's profound interest in and respect for modern psychiatry; but one will also find a much broader approach to life—one that gains in power and effectiveness from all of Dr. Liebman's diverse interests, one that embraces all experience, personal, familial, national, worldwide; psychology, philosophy, religion, literature, art, politics—all his passionate interests, and yet all of them focused by the striking integrity of his mind and character.

One of the outstanding virtues of his character was courage. Dr. Liebman never failed to face an issue directly, nor to examine without fear the evils of the world. As will be seen in many chapters of this book, it was his habit to look at any problem—be it moral, psychological, social, philosophical, or religious—to discern and describe its dangers and potentialities for evil, and then to give it a yea-saying answer. He called himself a "provisional optimist." He knew that combating evil was a serious business demanding both intellectual and emotional maturity. But he formed his answers by embracing life, not hiding from it, and he carried on the battle with joy and affirmation, and with a wonderful sense of humor that could lend balance and perspective to even the most serious of his thoughts.

Those of us who have worked with such inspirational material feel that *Hope for Man* represents the great and inspiring message he had to leave the world.

FAN LOTH LIEBMAN

Boston, Mass.
Summer, 1965

Contents

CHAPTER ONE

Hope for Man

Today's Pessimists
and How to Understand Them

In recent years there has been some discussion among scientists and philosophers about the Second Law of Thermodynamics —that principle in science which speaks of entropy, the gradual running down of the universe, the possibility that energy is being dissipated at a much more rapid rate than it is being built up, and that if this trend continues, within a billion or two billion years the whole earth will have grown cold and lifeless, the sun will have ceased emitting its life-giving rays, and the Ice Age will indeed have blanketed man and all of his works. Physicists and astronomers have debated the implications of this Second Law of Thermodynamics, and some authorities have argued that there is a constant creative process at work to balance the destructive and unwinding process going on in nature.

How academic and irrelevant seems a discussion about the death of the world and the coming of the Ice Age some billions of years hence, when many men, scientists and laymen alike, are speaking of the continuation of life under the threat of the atomic bomb! In our own time the Apocalyptic vision of the prophets of old may have been fulfilled, and the curtain will have fallen upon the human drama. Yes, I think it is correct to say that at no period in human history has there been such a sense of temporal urgency among men and women everywhere.

Time is short—very short. No wonder there is a dark pall over the literary and philosophical landscape of our day. The smoke of Hiroshima and Nagasaki has *not* been wafted away; it hangs like a fog over men's minds and hearts and spirits. In other centuries there was always the belief that time would solve many of the problems of pain and frustration and failure, but now time itself seems to have become an enemy of the human hope. The sand in the hourglass of our existence is running dangerously low, and many are the prophets who are calling attention to the fact that night is drawing near and threatening to shroud the earth in its burial garment.

Not that pessimism is a new phenomenon among men. It is probably as old as the first speculative thinkers. There always have been Cassandras anticipating destruction as the inevitable destiny of the human race. Hesiod and Ecclesiastes among the ancients, Schopenhauer and Nietzsche among the moderns, all spoke in foreboding accents, and sang their songs in a minor key. There have always been artists and thinkers prostrating themselves at the wailing wall of self-pity and social disaster.

Life itself certainly has offered plenty of data for the documentation of the pessimists: a flood here, an earthquake there, a great decimating plague somewhere else; all of the pursuing furies of natural catastrophes and wars, of love unrequited and ambition frustrated. Surely life has been very generous in offering the pessimists a cornucopia of disasters for their feasts of futility.

Perhaps the essential difference between the pessimist and the realist is that the former bows his head in resignation to the inevitability of evil, while the latter sees the darkness of experi-

ence as a challenge to him to fashion new lights which will conquer the shadows—new lights of science and medicine and law
to bind up the wounds and restrain the beast in the whims of
Nature and of human nature.

But this is getting a little ahead of our story. First, we must
understand the essential mood of pessimism. Pessimism negates
the hope of man by regarding the world as, at best, a product of
chance, a little island of matter afloat in a sea of meaninglessness, of empty space and dead stars. Pessimism looks upon the
whole human enterprise with jaundiced eyes and proclaims that
every human achievement is tainted with corruption and men-
aced by death. The pessimists proclaim that nothing is worthwhile, since all that we say and do and love will be engulfed ultimately by the equalizing grave, and our fondest dreams are
but masks that we place over the nightmare visage of reality.
Evaluating experience through dark-tinted spectacles of his own
making, the pessimist argues, often quite persuasively and con-
vincingly, that the whole world is a sheer product of chance, that
human society is a strenuous arena of competing and selfish wills
and that the individual himself is a battleground of passion and
pride, and on this battleground he and all he holds dear is destined to fall at last a casualty to the bullets of barbarism or
banality.

It is interesting and important to speculate about the different
types of pessimists and the sources of pessimism in the world. At
times one is tempted to believe that just as some people are born
phlegmatic and others volatile, so some people are born with
jaundiced vision, and others with open hearts and eagerness for
the joys as well as prepared to accept the frustrations of existence. Often, the pessimist seems to be a cool, skeptical, detached
thinker who has come to his conclusions on the basis of rational

reflection. But he is, more often than we suspect, a tortured product of a tortured environment who carries the scars of his childhood and adolescence as long as he lives. There is undeniable truth in the fact that many men and women who look always at the dark side of life are conditioned toward that vision by their private and personal frustrations and woundings, the warping loneliness of their own personal lives which they project into the loneliness of the universe.

Cannot the pessimist at times be viewed as the grown-up version of the little boy who takes delight in cutting the string of every balloon and watching the round globe of somebody's hopes float away into emptiness? We are all acquainted with people who seem to take a perverse delight in deflating everything around them, in tearing everyone else down to their own level of misery. In the gallery of pessimists are to be found many such human beings—the suspicious, who are always afraid of anything good and noble; the skeptical, who doubt that altruism and genuine love can really exist; the sad, who themselves have been so defeated in life and so disillusioned about its possibilities that they must make a philosophy of their private pains.

We can say, too, that the desperate optimists are those who need eternal reassurance about the goodness of life, and there are others who must hide their heads in the sand of comforting illusion. Perhaps these are men and women who have never outgrown their childish needs for a pat on the shoulder and the reassuring hug from father and mother; when they grow up, they look for other human beings and for the world itself to be their constant reassurance against anxiety. There are desperate optimists just as there are desperate pessimists among us.

Sometimes I think that the pessimists, considered in psychological terms, are adults who have never outgrown the need for punishment. Psychoanalysts have shown, by experiments and research, that every child at times needs both reassurance and needs punishment and will at moments provoke punishment as the lesser of two evils. The parental slap on the face often affords a release from unbearable guilt feelings and pent-up passion—a token of atonement and forgiveness.

Many a pessimist, it seems to me, is a person who still wants to be punished and for that reason creates a philosophy which is so despondent that it becomes like a flagellating whip. Although this may at first seem farfetched, I think there is more than a grain of truth in this understanding of pessimism. Many a dark and skeptical thinker, poet, or artist has expressed in the language of maturity many of the feelings and needs of childhood. Strange as it may seem at first, the philosophy of pessimism often serves a healing function for its creator, just as a child believes he will escape terrible punishment if he confesses his guilt to his parents, anticipating, therefore, the rejection or the disapproval of parents, or, by a kind of homeopathic magic, reducing the anger of the parent by self-reproach. Similarly, in many systems of pessimism we can find, if we search deeply enough, this anticipatory attack upon the universe. The thinker says the world is all evil, mankind is cruel, life is defeating and futile. By taking that approach to the universe he says to himself, in effect, "Nothing can ever surprise me, no punishment can ever startle me, no darkness can ever terrify me. I know it all in advance, and by knowing all in advance I am prepared to defeat the circle of enemies who surround me. I have disarmed the darkness by proclaiming it. I have carried the attack to the enemy, and by this maneuver I have conquered the enemy."

Pessimism, then, is sometimes a residue of the childish whims within us, the yearning for punishment, and the escape from guilt that comes with that punishment. We fashion our own verbal and philosophical whips to release ourselves from the guilt that we often feel. In the second place, pessimism is a strategy against surprise. If we paint a picture of life in the darkest colors, then no other painter can ever catch us unawares; and, knowing and proclaiming the worst about experience, we can enjoy the best that we encounter as an added gain, an unearned implement, a joyous reward for our realism.

Pessimism, therefore, is not merely "rational"; it is also emotional, reflecting one's whole life history. There are some people who seem to see better in the dark and who prefer the night with its jungle to the daytime with its garden. The unthinking optimist is a grown child afraid of bogeymen and ghosts, always wanting the reassurance of the sunlight. The dark pessimist, on the other hand, is the grown child who never got over the fact that he was placed in the closet; he believes, therefore, that the universe is a dark closet from which he can escape only if his sight has become adapted to the darkness. But light is more than ghosts and dark closets. It is both the sunlight and the evening star.

Much pessimism and optimism, then, are not what they seem to be; but are the residues and reflections of our psychological experience. The person who wishes to believe that all's right with the world and who keeps his gaze averted from the undeniable evils of life is, psychologically speaking, a personality who still yearns for the reassuring words of his father and mother.

There are, in fact, hysterical optimists who grow panic-stricken at the thought that something might be wrong with themselves or with life. I suspect that such individuals are afraid of the demonic destructive impulses within themselves. They build their philosophy of optimism into a wall which shields them from any recognition of the dark and unflattering aspects in their own natures and the possibility that they might give expression to aggressive and hostile deeds as well as fantasies. If God's in his heaven and all's right with the world, they feel they are shielded against brutality—including their own. Likewise, many persuasive pessimists can be understood only through depth psychology; they are combinations at times of impulses toward masochism, self-torture, and self-affliction on the one hand, and toward sadism, cruelty and callousness to others on the other hand.

Now, the fact that pessimism has its psychological roots in the soil of childhood is, of course, no refutation of the facts of evil and of the conflicts which this philosophy records. We who have lived through two tragic world wars, have seen the growth of the class struggle, have witnessed science being prosecuted more and more to the ends of destruction can well be excused for being impatient with the naïve optimism which, to a large degree, characterized the nineteenth century.

The dark philosophies of our day are inevitable reaction patterns against the blithe confidence in human progress which bemused our fathers and grandfathers. Not many decades ago people spoke of "the escalator of progress"; and there were many who were intoxicated with the dream of a Utopia around the corner. There was determinism in the realm of optimism just as in the realm of pessimism, and the nineteenth century saw many determinists of hope who had faith in the inevitability of the liberation of the human race through a little more education, a little more science, a little more technology. Man is innately good, proclaimed the naïve optimists not so long ago; man is a lover of reason, a builder of democracy, an architect of peace. Just give man a little more time and all of the dark stains of superstition and medieval oppression would disappear like clouds on a dark day driven away by the impatient sun.

Today all that naïve optimism seems to have an air of unreality about it. The idea that we human beings should just wait for the escalator of human progress to carry us to the summit of the mountain has been blasted by the bombs and shrapnel of the world wars of our age. We see how silly—how ridiculous—has been the fatalism involved in the idea of the inevitable progress and goodness and happiness. The critics have had a field day pointing out the manifold absurdities in the philosophy of optimism as it was expressed in the poetry of Browning and Tennyson, revealing all the superficiality of this comforting belief in man's reasonableness and goodness.

Today, after we have seen the human hells that man can design for his fellow creatures, it is not to be wondered at that the poets and artists are prophets of pessimism and spokesmen of cynicism. In fact, today one looks with suspicion upon an optimist as though he were not quite in his right mind, or perhaps as though he were still a little child masquerading in adult clothes. There is a hollow ring in the songs of triumph that men want to sing today, and many of the paintings of our century seem to be ashamed of themselves if they carry any recognizable message or meaning. A number of our painters seem most at home when they portray life as a charnel house and man either as a butcher or as a victim; the poets of our time are most at ease when they are playing with word symbols that have some private esoteric meaning for themselves and their little coterie of friends, and when their broken sentences convey at best a sense of heartbreak. The best poetry of our age is either a meaningless sigh, a groan, an elegy, or, among those who have tasted the challenge of religion, an incantation to a God whose unmerited grace may yet redeem the sinful earth from its just doom.

Our best novelists are most at home in scenes of violence, of lust, of cruelty, of oppression, and of war; their pages are stained with blood and tears. The literature of our twentieth century reeks with corruption, as if the stench of death had penetrated into the very ink with which the writers pen their lines and had permeated all the pages on which the testaments of youth and of old age are now being written.

Music, too, is full of discord and of dissonance; art consists of broken statues, malformed human figures, tangled legs and arms and grotesque skeletons garbed in surrealistic or impressionistic forms. Suspect in our age is the eye that sees beauty, the ear that hears harmony, the tongue that tastes any of the honey of love and friendship, achievement and hope.

Pessimism appears to be the profound truth which the sophisticated have learned to accept in contrast to their naïve brothers still playing in the sand of illusion. Pessimism, in effect, says that the eye should see the grotesque and the ugly, the ear should hear the clashing clamor of battlefields and the shrieking noises of factories, and the tongue should taste the bitter gall of private frustration and social oppression. This is the truth, say the pessimists. Remove the shutters from the windows of your minds, man, and look at life in all of its nakedness and see there the skeleton as it really is—the harsh angular lines, the shreds of flesh, the empty eye sockets of hope. Print that image indelibly upon your mind's eye, oh, man, and you will see the world as it is, and you will know your place in that world as a creature of a day, privileged, perhaps, to enjoy the lusts of the flesh and the delights of the tongue for but a moment. But a reckoning will come, and the accounting will be made, and you will realize, as did the pessimists of old, "Vanity of vanities . . . all is vanity."

Today's pessimists, of course, are not to be found only among the artists and the poets. At times everyone has a dark and sordid view of the world. No one can blame today's citizen for feeling gloomy at moments. The shrieking headlines of the newspapers convince us that we are living in a moment of enormous crisis—a crisis in which anything can happen, and out of which the worst indeed can emerge. We find many types of pessimists among the thinkers and leaders of our day. There are political and economic pessimists, and social philosophers who draw a very gloomy picture. The philosophical pessimists of our day outweigh, perhaps, both in number and in significance, the economic and the political pessimists.

Perhaps the greatest spokesman for darkness is the French playwright, novelist, and philosopher, Jean-Paul Sartre; he is creator of the movement called existentialism.

Perhaps Sartre would deny being a pessimist, but all those who follow in his footsteps are tarred with the black brush of negation. It is an interesting story. He and his friends were courageous heroes of the underground in France during World War II; they were leaders of the Resistance movement. But they lost all their belief in the traditions of their youth, in the church, in God, faith, and democracy, and they came out of the war sans illusions.

The philosophy of existentialism holds that man ultimately is alone in an absurd universe. Why he exists he does not and cannot know. There is no real purpose in his being. We are here, we know not why, and all that we can say is that we ought to live our lives, in spite of the total absurdity of the universe, with as much dignity and responsibility as we can muster. Man is ultimately alone, and no one can remove him from that aloneness. In his isolation, however, each individual carries the burden of moral responsibilities with him as long as he lives. He must act not in accordance with convention or in response to external pressure, but in accordance with his subjective decisions. Nothing outside man is of any real significance. It is only his own existence that is primary and fundamental and vital.

Sartre is the prophet of a stoic atheism, a proclamation of human courage and heroism in the face of nothingness and universal absurdity. His play *No Exit* is a good illustration of his essential outlook. It tells the story of three people who are shown into a hotel bedroom in Hell. We learn that one girl is actually the betrayer of her husband, the cause of his death. Another girl is an abnormal creature, also responsible for the destruction of life upon earth. The third character in this drama is a man who, when the testing hour came, had proved himself to be a coward, escaping and fleeing from his duty. All three are sentenced to exist in this room without any exits—no windows, no doors—condemned to spend eternity together.

In this very vivid drama Sartre draws his picture of human nature as he sees it. These three people are the torturers of one another. They find that they cannot escape from each other, and yet they cannot live with each other. They remain what they were during their lifetimes: cruel, evil, sadistic, narcissistic, self-loving and weak. One of the women says in this drama, "You are—your life and nothing else." This is the philosophy of existentialism. The pessimism of Sartre is revealed in the brilliant statement where the man says, "So this is Hell. I'd never have believed it. Do you remember all we were told about the torture chambers, the fire and brimstone? There's no need for red-hot pokers. Hell is—other people!"

Where does Sartre's philosophy stem from? What is the basis for his insistence upon the absurdity of existence, and at the same time upon the duty of the individual to achieve a path of his own? He is a spiritual descendant of the greatest source of pessimism in our age, the Danish theologian Søren Kierkegaard, who died over a hundred years ago. A Kierkegaard cult has developed in intellectual circles; and in many respects it is a cult of darkness, anxiety and negation. Who was this Kierkegaard? What did he write and teach? The story itself has a fascinating place in the history of ideas. Kierkegaard's father was a poor peasant who went to Copenhagen and made a fortune for himself. In their mature years, the father and his wife lived under a shadow as a result, as they believed, of some early blasphemy against God. In the last decades of his life the elder Kierkegaard spent his waking hours in study and conversation and religious reflection, always attempting to expiate the sins of his blasphemy.

It was in this morbid parental atmosphere that young Søren grew up. As a child he was exposed to theological conversation and was made conscious of the weight on his shoulders of the world and its sinfulness. As a young man, Søren lived the life of a typical son of wealthy parents, educated and cultured, enjoying the delights of the flesh and the pleasures of high spirits. This period of revolt against his father, however, soon gave way to a very deep identification with his father's mood. Then Kierkegaard fell in love with a beautiful young girl named Regine; after their engagement had been announced, however, he was conscience-stricken. Feeling unworthy and unable to go through with the marriage, he broke the engagement, entered a school of theology and prepared himself for the life of a religious thinker and teacher and writer. After his father's death,

Kierkegaard inherited his estate, and, while living a very comfortable bourgeois existence, surrounded by all the luxuries and beauties available to a man of wealth, he began publishing, at first under pseudonyms, a number of philosophical, ethical and religious books.

The books created a tremendous stir in literary and philosophical circles; here was a man brave enough to attack the idols of philosophy, to speak scornfully about Kant and Hegel and all the scientific philosophers concerned with the problems of external reality and the objects of nature, a man who proclaimed that the real task of man was to find the way to his inner self, pointing out that "what is true is true for me," that it is the subjective, not the objective, truth that is important, and that man's primary concern is with his own existence, not with the essence of the universe or the essence of nature.

Kierkegaard never married. He carried on a very pleasant existence in Copenhagen, but his real life was spent in his study with his books and manuscripts. More and more it became obvious to the citizens of Denmark that here was an original mind, an iconoclast. Kierkegaard did not hesitate to express his personal opinion in brilliant and beautiful books, often very deep and complex in structure. He went to the extreme of attacking organized Christianity, as he saw it, as a kind of hypocrisy and superstition. Eventually, Kierkegaard came to feel that the Christian clergy around him, while very nice, decent, good-hearted men, were certainly not Christians in the deeper sense of the term. As a matter of fact, no one was a Christian, so far as he knew, because Christianity demanded of the Christian something extraordinary in the way of sacrifice: the sacrifice of intellectual and rational consistency, and the leap of faith into the arms of a paradoxical God. Vigorously and brilliantly he attacked the official representatives of Christendom, and dared to say that there were no real Christians in ecclesiastical circles.

While the controversy over this courageous and heretical position was raging, Kierkegaard became ill and died at the age of forty-two. He left the world some thirteen volumes of poetry, philosophy and theology. For many decades after his death, his name remained shrouded in obscurity; it is only in recent times that his books have been rescued from oblivion. Now the whole English-speaking world—at least the intellectual part of that world—has become acquainted with the world view of this Socrates among modern theologians.

What is it in essence that he teaches? Perhaps the word "teaches" is incorrect in this connection; Kierkegaard's writing was not done systematically, but rather in the form of diaries and symposia, almost in the manner of the dialogues of Plato, and in the forms of confessions and reflections. He was no architect of a dull, pedestrian, systematic philosophy. He wrote at times like a playwright, at other times like a poet. He was fond of the beautiful metaphor, the anecdote, the musical and literary illustration. He was a very vivid writer; all his books are a kind of confession, an autobiography of the mind and soul. He wrestled with himself constantly, trying to understand why he had broken off his engagement to his beloved Regine, justifying his loveless state, trying also to clarify his relationship with his father and his father's sinfulness. He traveled a lonely odyssey seeking the truth—the truth that would be true for him—and in his quest for salvation he came at last to a unique and profound understanding of the Christian faith.

Kierkegaard made a number of very brilliant observations. He pointed out, for example, that the realm of the aesthetic (which is the realm of beauty and art and all things that are sensuously appealing and at the same time transitory) is in a sense the realm of youth and which gives way to the realm of the ethical, which to him is symbolized by marriage with all its stability and its pedestrian mutuality.

He spoke with great understanding of the mutual devotion of husband and wife, of the sense of wholeness that comes to human beings in their ethical obligations to each other in marriage —but then he says, "This is not for me." From the realm of the ethical, which to him is prosaic and pedestrian, Kierkegaard proceeds at last into the realm of the religious. He finds that the way of religion is not comforting or consoling; it is a dark and risky journey, this journey of the religious soul, accompanied by much intense suffering and pain and many obstacles and valleys of doubt. The religious realm is the realm of faith, and by faith Kierkegaard means a leap into the irrational, the absurd, the paradoxical. That realm of faith cannot be justified by the commonsense logical processes of daily living. Kierkegaard brooded much over the story of Abraham and the sacrifice of Isaac, and found in this remarkable story from the Book of Genesis the essence of the religious experience. Now, natural morality commands a father to love and protect his son, but, lo and behold, here the voice of God commands Abraham to slay his beloved Isaac. By every criterion of reason this act would make the patriarch a murderer. Furthermore, Abraham had been promised by God that through Isaac, his son, the seed of Israel would become great upon the earth. Now, that promise apparently was to be erased completely by the death of his heir. And yet there was the patriarch, with all the promises of God ringing in his ears, his natural fatherly feelings, outraged by this demand, ascending the mountain with his son, his knife ready for the slaughter. That act of sacrifice by the father, Kierkegaard felt,

27

was the true act of faith, because at that moment Abraham was going counter to everything that was rational. He took his leap into the unknown, almost into the unbelievable. He proved himself a believer in God by turning his back upon common sense and the ordinary dictates of a father's conscience, and accepting blindly and obediently the authoritative commandment of the Lord.

This motif of a leap into the irrational and the absurd Kierkegaard (in his great philosophic work entitled *Concluding Unscientific Postscript*) justified as an approach to the universe. In this very long book the Danish thinker mercilessly attacked the objective philosophers and scientists of his own time and of earlier history by saying that their work in a certain sense was trivial and unimportant. They dealt only with the categories of that which is measurable, that which is visible, and that which is tangible. They were concerned with proving our knowledge of the stars and the rocks, of the stones and the colors of the outer world; but all these objective philosophers ignored the true essence of the problem of life which is man himself, man in his inwardness, man in his subjectivity. This is the existential problem which no one of the philosophers building the great towering system of metaphysics had ever come to understand. The one philosopher in history who did understand it was Socrates, for he was always concerned with finding out the truth for himself and with exposing the truth for those of his disciples and followers who could understand him. But Socrates was not interested in imposing his conclusions upon anyone; he was only being the "midwife" to other people's thoughts, thus enabling thinkers to come to their subjective truths, to their inward light. "The object is not to know the truth, but to be it."

Kierkegaard entered more and more into the religious realm.

For him God became more and more of a reality, as did the separation between man and God: Every human being, he said, is a sinner, lost in darkness and despair. A man begins to be religious when he resigns himself to his inevitable limitations, and begins to suffer the tortures of anguish at the thought of his own nothingness and helplessness before God. Just at the moment when he is about to be annihilated by his own self-abasement, when he realizes that his evil cuts him off from real communion with God that he is filled as a vessel is filled with all the waters of guilt—at that very moment God comes to man with the cup of grace, redeems him from total despair, and draws him back from the abyss of annihilation.

Life, as Kierkegaard saw it, is not something that is lived actually in the world of material reality among all the unimportant social pleasures and distractions of the daily routine. Nor is life lived at its best among the retorts and the test tubes of laboratories. Life has meaning for an individual only when he discovers his real destiny and his real despair, when he begins to be aware of his finiteness and of the shadow of death that is over all his works. Then and then only, at that moment of terrible despair and dread, there comes the assurance of God's helpfulness and grace. The eternal breaks into the temporal. The infinite God rescues finite man from his terrible anxiety and his original sins.

Kierkegaard was undoubtedly the anatomist of anxiety and anguish *par excellence*. No one in modern times has described so impressively the spiritual torments of man as he confronts his own destiny, his sense of aloneness, his feeling of isolation from mankind and society, his feeling of being a cut flower divorced from the roots of reality, namely, God. If you grant Kierkegaard's premises, you are swept along by the majestic poetry of his prose, the vividness of his imagery, and the persuasiveness of his argument. He knew full well the temptations of life. He described love and human passion and the sensual and erotic realm as well as a novelist could. He brought into his religious books many unforgettable characters: businessmen and judges, clergymen, artists, musicians, actors, women and men in all conditions of sinfulness and saintliness. His books contain a whole gallery of human prototypes, and his philosophy is expressed in the most emotionally stirring language that one could possibly wish for.

The essence of his thought is that man is ultimately alone —alone with God—and that all other forms of relatedness are just illusory. We get so caught up in all kinds of enterprises, legal, ecclesiastical and philosophical, that we waste our short day on earth on such unimportant problems as money or fame, or on the acquisition of knowledge and power in the mastery of nature. All of this, to his mind, was relatively insignificant in comparison to the essential questions of man: Who am I? What am I? What is my duty? What is my destiny? How can I make my peace with God?

Kierkegaard pointed out some of the forms of pride that make men and nations sin: pride of nation, pride of class, pride of position. All external possessions and all external truths are of no significance compared with the inward truth which man alone can discover for himself. The duty of man is to find himself and to seek himself as long as he lives, to know that he is under the sentence of death from the moment that he is born. When he becomes sufficiently aware of his fragility and his frailties and of the corruption that eats away at his heart, and when he realizes that there is a vast chasm that separates him from God, and he despairs deeply enough and is tortured inwardly enough, then and then alone can he make the leap that will carry him into the arms of the Divine and that will give him at least before his death the possibility of a little foretaste of the paradise that will come through irrational nonlogical faith.

Kierkegaard argued that there is no salvation for the individual in all of the works of social reform and better government and loftier democracy; all these, again, are mere manipulations of material reality which are empty of significance when weighed in the scale of Divinity. Existence is not logical, and human life is not logical. Each person can be understood only in himself and not by an outsider. Man is nothing, absolutely nothing, before the presence of God. It is when a man comes to realize his terrible burden of guilt that he achieves for the first time the possibility of some grace from the hands of God.

Kierkegaard's was a very provocative and striking intellect, whether we agree or disagree with his conclusions. He did not try to justify his outlook upon life by "sweet reasonableness"; as a matter of fact, he took just the opposite course and proclaimed that faith is true by the willingness of man to act on that which seems to be absurd and irrational, that which transcends our limited little vision. Kierkegaard was a follower of Job as well as of Socrates, maintaining that inward truth is worth all the outer knowledge that we can ever accumulate and certainly is worth all the material possessions that we can ever aggregate.

There are many beautiful things in Kierkegaard's writings. I can mention here only a few of the passages which strike me as outstanding and brilliant: "One must know one's self before knowing anything else." . . . "I cannot forget myself even when I am asleep." . . . "The whole of existence frightens me, from the smallest fly to the mystery of the incarnation." . . . "My doubt is terrible." . . . "There are many people who reach their conclusions about life like schoolboys; they cheat their master by copying the answer out of a book without having worked out the sum for themselves."

Kierkegaard despised the objective scientific approach to the world, regarding it as prosaic and pedestrian, lacking all personal color and all subjective truth. The very accusation which many modern philosophers make against artists—namely, that they are biased and subjective—becomes a great blessing in the eyes of Kierkegaard. A detached thinker was no thinker as far as he was concerned.

Kierkegaard believed that even in loving another person one must be sufficient unto one's self. Here is the essential motif in his whole thought, namely, his contempt for human relatedness and his emphasis on self-sufficient isolation and essential aloneness. He was in a way a kind of spiritual masochist enjoying his pain.

Kierkegaard was a provocative and profound thinker, one of the supreme individualists in the whole history of thought. He is no man to read if you want a logical and consistent system of thought. His categories of truth are not the usual philosophic categories of substance and form and potentiality and actuality; rather they are personal and individualistic categories of passion and feeling, of love and hate, guilt and suffering, doubt and faith. He is no respecter of conventional truths. He shocks and horrifies and frightens. To read him after reading some of the conventional philosophers is like taking a bath in an icy-cold brook.

One could say that in all of his books Kierkegaard wrote a confession of his own inadequacies and perturbations. He had no use for science or for society. His was a lonely, isolated, haunted mind, twisted and distorted by his parents' gloom. He was never convinced of the naturalness and normality of family love and human relationship and relatedness. None of the social virtues are to be found in him. He had no room in his religious life for fellowship and friendship and the community as a mirror of the Divine. He was no rebel against the economic and political evils of his day. He was an authoritarian proclaiming the necessity of the absolute obedience to the will of God and submission to the mystery of God. There is no doubt that he was exceedingly vain and arrogant in daring to pit his intellectual conclusions against all the doctrines and dogmas of his day. From the standpoint of social amelioration he was a conservative, even a reactionary. He was perfectly willing to let things take care of themselves as far as social and political arrangements were concerned. Yet, diagnose him as one may—as a neurotic, a tortured soul haunted by guilt feelings and unresolved parental conflict, a lonely pilgrim adrift on a lonely sea—and analyze him psychiatrically and psychologically as one will, one must recognize that here was a seminal intellect, a great artist, a magnificent poet, and a profound psychologist; he gave the world one of the best analyses of human anxiety and human anguish, and the sense of the burdens and pains of man as an individualistic thinker. He remains one of the great spiritual and philosophic doubters searching out new horizons.

He is the Hamlet spirit in the modern world eternally echoing the question "To be or not to be." He is one of the great ancestors of today's pessimists; he saw life as essentially dark, a jungle of passions and lusts, fears and angers, lighted only by the few luminous gleams that come to us from a source other than this world, from the radiant luminary of the Divine.

There are other spiritual grandfathers of today's pessimists—Nietzsche and Schopenhauer, Ibsen and Kafka. Ibsen's famous drama, *The Wild Duck,* is the source of much of the modern philosophy of illusion. As a matter of fact, all those thinkers of our times who speak of life as an illusion, and whose cheerless message to mankind is that we have to live as if there were ideals and values and truths to be attained and to be preserved, but that all of this really is just wishful thinking—the whole thesis that is elaborated, for example, in Eugene O'Neill's *The Iceman Cometh*—all go back to the motif created many decades ago by Ibsen. In *The Wild Duck* one of the characters, Relling, makes very clear this dark and "realistic" approach to human experience. He attacks another character, Gregers, because he is afflicted with "that plaguey integrity fever," and when Relling is questioned about what remedy he is applying to a person so sick as himself, he replies, "My usual one—I am cultivating the life-illusion in him." "Life-illusion?" asks Gregers. "Yes, I said illusion." And Relling later explains, "Rob the average man of his life-illusion, and you rob him of his happiness at the same stroke."

This motif of life as an illusion runs through much of modern philosophy and poetry and other literature. It reveals itself in Sartre and the existentialist movement. Sartre, of course, goes back to Kierkegaard as well as to the more contemporaneous philosophers of Germany, Heidegger and Jaspers, who rebelled against the objectivity and abstractionism of contemporary science and philosophy. They, too, proclaimed a gospel of human anxiety, human aloneness and the shadow of death which hangs over each individual every moment that he breathes.

A most important influence and source of pessimism in our day is Franz Kafka. Just as there is a Kierkegaard cult in the present intellectual world, so there is a Kafka cult. Kafka lived in the Austria of the First World War; he died in 1924. His father, a successful merchant, was a dominating personality who tyrannized all the members of his household. Young Franz was terrified of his father as well as reverential toward him. Kafka wrote once about his father, "From your armchair you ruled the world. Your opinion was the right one; every other was crazy, exaggerated, abnormal."

Kafka never escaped from the spell of his dominating father. When his father wanted him to go into business, and he wanted to become an artist, he compromised by going into business and writing in his spare hours. He was forced by his father to wear very old-fashioned clothing, and he never seemed at home either in his clothes or in the world around him. He was an awkward personality, shy, introverted, afraid. He envied his father's strength, but he never could achieve his virility.

This consciousness of his failure haunted him all his life. He became engaged—as Kierkegaard did—and remained engaged for five years; but when he developed a tubercular cough he felt relieved, he later confessed, for this removed from him the obligation to go through with the marriage. More and more Kafka withdrew into himself. He had a small circle of friends, some of them Zionists in the Austrian capital, who attempted to convince him of the validity of Zionism. He studied Hebrew literature and tried to familiarize himself with the Talmud. All during this time he was writing short stories and fragments of novels; and in this fiction Kafka revealed a genius of mind, a great, authentic, lonely voice.

In one of his most important novels, *The Castle*, the leading character has been asked to come to a village to work as a land surveyor for the authorities of the castle. He goes to the castle but is refused admission, and is even denied the privilege of settling in the village. As the novel continues, the central character

35

is continually frustrated in his efforts to cut through the bureaucratic red tape and to get to the very throne room, as it were, of the castle. He wants to receive acceptance from the authorities, to be given permission to fulfill his role as a surveyor and to find his happiness among the villagers. But no matter how he tries, he is always defeated. He is turned back; obstacles are put in his way. He is made to feel an outsider, an alien, a pariah, an outcast, lonely and forlorn.

The characters in Franz Kafka's novels are anonymous, nameless. They have initials, but no full names. Orphans of the universe, they seem to dwell in a kind of no-man's-land. Kafka's novels are works of art, depicting human aloneness in a most brilliant and penetrating fashion. His characters are tortured and haunted, always cut off from significant communication, always striving for unity. In his story "The Great Wall of China," the people try to escape from their egocentricity into a communal identity, a collective happiness and collective salvation, but Kafka never achieved this kind of collective warmth and mutual relatedness. All his life he was a lonely man, haunted by guilt feelings, hating his father, striving to identify with and to possess some of the strength of his father, yet crushed by his father's strength. He never possessed the faith of Kierkegaard, whom he in some ways resembled and whom he admired very much, for he could not take the leap into the unknown and into the irrational. He never felt the arms of God around him. He knew only the sense of guilt, sinfulness, separation and isolation. His characters are ciphers, skeletons; and his main theme is, as someone has put it, "the helplessness of man before the superior powers of our mechanical civilization, the bureaucracy of our inhuman world." Kafka was a deflated individual, and all the main characters in his novels are also deflated individuals, empty of significance, devoid of value—a problem to themselves and a question mark to the society in which they precariously live.

These are some of the ancestors and sources of today's pessimists. The existentialists of France and their disciples are the heirs of Kierkegaard and Ibsen and Kafka, to mention but a few of the elegists of emptiness, the men who see life as a burden and not as a blessing, a problem and not a solution. They see the human soul alone in the universe, exposed to starvation and death.

One cannot dismiss lightly the writings of Kierkegaard and Kafka and Sartre. It would be easy to ridicule many of the extreme statements made by the existentialists of our day; the practical man is always ready with a witty remark and a scornful sneer for the visions and dreams of the poet, the philosopher, the abstract thinker. The pessimist might well say to many a modern man and woman, "At least I look at the world with honesty and candor. I see all the evil under the sun, and I have glimpsed without flinching the pain and the tragedy inherent in the human story. You, however, live your life totally on the surface of things. You are concerned about your social position, your food and your money, your possessions, your security. Occasionally you give a thought to some problems of political or international reforms. Where are you different, actually, from the animals of the fields who also are absorbed in the acquisition of food and the preservation of their skins, and in all the things concerned with survival? The ants in the ant heap are very busy. You say that you are busy, caught up in the details of your daily routine. In that regard you are no different from the ants or the bees. You and the squirrels are blood brothers, hoarding possessions for the wintry season yet to come. In some ways you might resemble a vulture, a beast of prey, who pounces upon his help-less victim as you do upon your victims in your social circle or in your employee group. Wherein, then, are you different from the beasts of the fields and the birds of the air? You are different only if you exercise your mind to think thoughts and formulate ideas which no animal can formulate—the thoughts and ideas of man and the mysterious universe around him and the shadow of death over him. I, the pessimist, come as your liberator to free you from your bondage to superficiality, to liberate you from the chains of convention. Do not stone me but welcome me, because I make you think. Thought, though it may not give you happiness, can bless you with serenity."

Existentialism in one respect is an appealing and persuasive doctrine just because of its brave honesty and its open-eyed real-ism. Sartre, in essence, proclaims that modern man evades re-sponsibility for his own deeds and that there are many conspira-tors aiding him in this escape from moral decision. How many of us, for example, rely on the state or the government or the church, not only to make up our minds for us, but to do what we ourselves ought to do? In this complex and bewildering society of which we are a part, there is always a seductive temptation to flee from the burden of maturity. The very vastness of the world excuses us from personal decision, and we feel a great inner relief when we say, "God will take care of this"—or the govern-ment, or the President. It is this escape from responsibility which existentialism rejects. It tells us that man cannot look to God or to the state or to the class to solve his problems, but that each individual in his aloneness is both privileged and burdened with the necessity of making his own decision; that decision, the existentialist tells us, determines his life for good or for evil. This is, no doubt, a kind of modern stoicism, but at least it does bestow upon the human being a dignity of which he has been robbed by the vast impersonality of the twentieth century with its herd movements, its class struggles, its religious and ecclesiastical submission.

The modern pessimists, then, call upon each individual to be himself, or, more properly speaking, to become himself. The existentialists, from Kierkegaard and Heidegger to Sartre, really want to serve a purpose, namely, to awaken man from the sleep of intellectual and moral and spiritual death. They want to arouse men from a condition of smugness, complacency and inner numbness, to remove them from the false or superficial situations in which they live and spend their days, and to bring them face to face with the ultimate condition of man which is that of a lonely individual set down upon the seashore of life for a few brief hours in the sunlight and in the shadow before the tide comes in and he is swept away, carried out to the sea of eternity. The existentialists feel that during those brief days on the shore of time, man should spend his hours and his energy not in building crumbling little houses of sand, or in collecting seashells of wealth or power or fame, but, rather, in confronting himself and the naked horizon of the universe, and finding his meaning and his place in the infinite spaces embracing him.

There is something profound and persuasive in this doctrine of existentialism. It is quite true that modern man is caught up in a roaring tempest of routine and spends his waking hours in a merry-go-round of triviality and meaninglessness. Sometimes it seems to me many of us are in a dangerous situation: we are spiritually paralyzed, and intellectually and morally numbed. When we go to a physician and he tests our reflexes with his little hammer, if our knees do not bounce we know something is definitely wrong. Spiritually we are in that condition when our reflexes do not work; and we have become numb and the skins of our souls, as it were, no longer react sensitively to all of the stimuli of values and dreams and thoughts and ideals. The paralytic who sits in his chair immobile with fixed and stony eye, with rigid cheek and motionless hand, might very well be taken as the symbol of twentieth-century man similarly paralyzed within by all of the tensions and conflicts of the twentieth century, with a heart, many times, of stone, an immobile mind, a rigid imagination.

Much of our life is lived on the surface, and seldom, if ever, do we penetrate to the depths of existence. When man is in the presence of catastrophe or crisis, sometimes for a moment or two he plumbs the depths within himself. The individual then asks himself, What meaning is there to my being? What is the significance of this great mystery? Here am I, surrounded by mystery, bound to this universe as if by an umbilical cord. I am alone . . . I really do not know other people. Their surfaces I know, but their real depths I can never penetrate, even as I do not penetrate the mysteries and depths of myself. But here I am; I exist. Existentially, I live an isolated existence, separated even from wife and children, for I and no one else feel the burden and the blessing of my being, and just as I was born alone, so shall I die alone. Still, while I live, I can face the crises and catastrophes of life maturely and stoically.

I remember the story of Conrad's great novel, *Lord Jim*—the story of a man who, after experiencing cowardice and betraying his code, went to his death affirmatively. I know many stories of young soldiers and sailors who have gone to their deaths heroically and stoically, stories of civilians whose heroic acts redeem man of all of the taints of selfishness and barbarism. The fireman who rescues a child at the risk of his own life, the policeman who humbly fulfills his duty often at the cost of his life—these peacetime heroes are symbols of men of decision who, by their acts, affirm the dignity of the human race.

It is not the catastrophes and crises of life which are truly important, but rather the way the individual faces those catastrophes and crises. Existentialism speaks a great deal about the absurdity of life. By this it means that the great problems of existence are not to be found in the social and pragmatic realms, are not solved by a little tinkering here or there with some phase of economics or politics. The great problems of life are profoundly individualistic—the way we face the nothingness and the meaninglessness of the universe and yet assert in the face of that absurdity our own essential moral dignity and responsibility.

These prophets of pessimism can, indeed, lead men to despair or to atheism, but they can also lead men to greater sensitivity. Their words and thoughts often are like the physician's little hammer testing our spiritual reflexes; they make us know whether we are numb and paralyzed within or alert to the mystery and also the majesty of the universe and our place in it. Pessimism is a challenge to the superficial optimism which lulls human beings into complacency and a kind of sleep of death. Optimism at times can become like a blinding snowstorm in which we wander, sinking even deeper into snowdrifts of uncritical belief and uncriticized confidence; there is danger that we shall lie down in the snow in its deceptive warmth, until we are embraced at last prematurely by death. Pessimism stirs us from such an unthinking optimism and from the tragic superficiality and banality in which we so often spend our days. Too numerous are the men and women who come to the grave without ever really having lived deeply.

Pessimism also makes us wary of our illusions and armors us

41

against future disillusionment. A man who says to himself, "I know all the tragedies and evils, the doubts and the despairs to which human flesh is heir" has armored himself against many future pains which catch the unawakened by surprise. Pessimism places us on guard against naïve confidence, unreflected optimism, unthinking superficiality.

Certainly there is enormous evil in the world to document the pessimist's evaluation of human experience. Certainly, at times, we all feel like Ivan in *The Brothers Karamazov*, who wanted to give back his entrance ticket to life because the world involved suffering for the innocent and he found life on those conditions intolerable. The pessimistic thesis that life is all tragic, all evil, all worthless, is, however, one that should not be accepted uncritically. The pessimist tells a partial truth about experience but not the total truth—for if there is a problem of evil in the world, there is also good in the world. If we confront disorder, chaos, cruelty, callousness, we also confront beauty, harmony, order, love, tenderness. The landscape of experience is never painted in one color; it is splashed with many colors, dark and bright, at one and the same time.

What hope, then, is there for man? If man is, as the pessimist many times asserts, inevitably selfish, inevitably cruel, inevitably aggressive; if it is true that men and women are by nature condemned to a kind of inescapable competitiveness and hatred, and are doomed by their very essence to go to war, to tear down and to destroy—if this indeed is the truth about man, then we have to face it courageously and honestly.

I do not believe, however, that pessimism tells the whole story. The philosopher Sidney Hook has pointed out that there is a tendency when we are confronted by some outrageous human action to exclaim, "This is what man is *really* like." This is a judgment that people rarely make when human beings display great devotion and heroism. Yet there is no reason why we should not say in the presence of nobility. "*This* is what man is really like." The truth is that under one set of circumstances man acts belligerently and callously, and under another set of conditions acts nobly and self-sacrificingly. The task of human intelligence is not to fold our hands and sit by patiently and passively awaiting doom; it is rather to use our reason to find out what the circumstances are in which we will cooperate, and what the circumstances are in which men destroy and tear each other to pieces.

Science today certainly does not justify the pessimistic conclusion. Some years ago, the great anthropologist Ruth Benedict, analyzing human nature on the basis of her vast experience, came to the conclusion that belligerence and aggressiveness are not universal aspects of the human race. Actually, they are late arrivals on the human scene. For tens of thousands of years men lived without weapons or warfare. Even in contemporary primitive societies, men are not always war-oriented. The truth about man is his infinite plasticity. He is capable of fashioning heavens or hells. Man can use power to destroy one another, or they can laugh and sing and work together. There is nothing inherently destructive or aggressive in human nature which cannot be tamed. There is no congenital war-mindedness in the genes of the human species. In this connection the testimony of Warder C. Allee, professor of zoology of the University of Chicago, in a study on human nature, points out that Darwin was wrong about "the survival of the fittest"; that animal life is actually governed by a law that reads "cooperate or die." Even animals must form some sort of community in order to survive. Human tendencies toward goodness on personal, community, national and international levels are as natural as man's trend toward being intelligent. Social life is not an accident. It is a normal and basically widespread phenomenon. The cooperative forces in nature are stronger than the antisocial forces. If this were not true, there could never have been evolution from the simpler to the more complex forms of animals and of human beings. In other words science today does not agree that man is doomed to cruelty, competitiveness and mutual destruction.

Moreover, we have all seen human beings perform acts which bring satisfaction not only to themselves but to others. Self-interest is, it is true, part of our makeup, but in satisfying ourselves we also often help others. The progress man has made through his intelligence and through science means that human nature can change and grow and develop. We are now at the very threshold of a world situation where, if we use our reason adequately, we can create a society of such abundance and such security for all of the family of the earth that there need be no future war, and all the competitive selfishness which has stained and marred the human story from the beginning of time will wither away.

Hopelessness about human nature is not justified because, just as the world's landscape has enormously changed with the coming of physical and chemical science, so the inner landscape of man has changed and can change further with the development of the sciences of society and psychology. As Professor Barrows Dunham points out in his book *Man Against Myth,* "When mankind has attained a state in which goods and services abound and exploitation has ceased, there will be no social reason why your welfare should be incompatible with mine. Selfishness, having no longer anything important to do, will wither away, taking our problems with it. . . . The human race, which abolished slavery and serfdom, which learned and practiced political democracy, cannot be eternally thwarted of control over its entire social destiny. It may appear a fabled and Utopian dream, but dreams far more fabled and Utopian have come true. . . . The dreams men dream while waking can become the substance of a world."

In this atomic age, abundance, social cooperation and world peace are possible, and there is nothing that changeable and changing man cannot create, once he has determined upon a creative course of action. True, we may go through recessions and economic depressions if we are subject to blindness and folly. We may, if we are not wise enough, destroy one another in an atomic war, but this is by no means inevitable. The thesis that either we must bomb Russia or Russia will bomb us, because two such great powers cannot live together in the same world in a kind of balance of power, is absolutely negated by the story of our own country. In the United States the two great forces of capital and labor do live together, with struggles and with differences of opinion, to be sure, and with certain inevitable conflicts, yet they coexist. Similarly, Russia and America can and must live together in an international balance of power under the United Nations leading to world government and world law.

Pessimism dooms us in advance by its philosophy of hopelessness, and of waiting for the midnight hour to strike. It is true that we may be doomed if mankind does not use its reason and intelligence to achieve salvation together. We say, however, that the destruction of all mankind is not inevitable. Mankind *may* be doomed, but it *will* be doomed if it surrenders to defeatism in advance, a defeatism that does not recognize that men can plan together the great social adventure, the winning of justice and abundance, security, and peace for the human family.

Today's pessimists sing the song of man's aloneness. In this twentieth century, they have lost a simple faith in God, and have found that all their substitute gods—whether class or nation or race—have proved to be idols with clay feet. And so there has grown up in our age an enormous agnosticism and atheism, not merely about the God in heaven, but also about all the deities on earth, all the pathways to salvation which have given men relief in the past. The essence of the point of view of the existentialists, and of Kafka and Kierkegaard, is that man is a lonely atom condemned to be a prisoner in the cell of the universe, face to face with nothingness, consumed with anxiety and dread, when he thinks of the sword of death hanging every moment over his head. The world that he confronts is vast, and he himself is meaningless. We are all of us racing toward death and doom. While we live, only personal integrity is worth while; it gives us whatever transitory meaning we can find in the human journey.

Does this seem adolescent? Well, the adolescent often asks profound questions which the adult forgets or represses. As adults we become so involved and so busy, so like ants or bees in our daily routines of getting and spending, that we forget the deepest questions of poetry and philosophy. Like Pascal we are in our essence alone, confronting "the silence of these infinite spaces," anxious and anguished because at the core of our beings, in spite of all of the buildings and the skyscrapers, the automobiles and the radios around us, and even our dear ones and families—we are born alone, we live alone, we die alone. We are small, valueless ciphers; no voices and no sounds ever reach us. We are alone forever on the shore of eternity.

This is the mood of modern pessimism: the elegy of humanity, the swan song of despair, the epitaph of hope. Here is the doctrine of man's valuelessness and unrelatedness. Was man always so conscious of his aloneness? Was there ever a time when man felt himself significant, a creature of purpose, a child of the Divine? What is our human destiny as the great teachers and poets, the religionists and the philosophers of the ages have conceived it? How can we escape the prison cell of our isolation? How can we find the building stones of life that will enable us to transform the wailing wall of darkness into a great altar and temple of triumph? These are the questions which we must attempt to answer as we seek the solution to the challenges and the problems that pessimism raises in our time and in our minds.

CHAPTER TWO

What Is Our Human Destiny?

HISTORICAL SURVEY

The world of today, as we have come to see, more often than not regards man as a zero, a cipher. Man has lost his significance; the key words in literature and philosophy are "aloneness" and "alienation." Men feel themselves to be only little creatures lost among the giant skyscrapers of our city and in the vast emptiness of our space. That, perhaps, is the appeal of the tramp in Charlie Chaplin's movies and of all the little men portrayed in the movies and the dramas of the twentieth century. On the mass-communication level, the appeal of many programs is to the feeling of bewilderment and confusion, the rather forced laughter and strained humor which Professor Abram Kardiner analyzes brilliantly in *The Psychological Frontiers of Society*. All these reflections of modern man's inner confusion and sense of being lost and lonely in a meaningless universe, an uncaring world, make us ask with desperate urgency, "What is our human destiny?" Has it always been true that man has felt himself a displaced person in a universe that has something of the semblance of a barracks room? Have people always had the sense of solitary confinement in the narrow prison cells of their own beings, of hunger for relatedness and companionship and

48

status and value? In other ages did man regard himself as something more than a zero and a spiritual cipher? To find the answer to these important questions we must turn to the immortals in literature and philosophy to discern their portrait of human nature and human destiny.

In the Hebrew Bible we see man regarded as the child of God created in the Divine image, erring and errant, but nevertheless the center of creation. Throughout the books of the Bible we find a brilliant and coherent philosophy of history, a point of view that certainly clothed man with dignity, and with value, in spite of his sinfulness and waywardness. We have learned, in other words, that the writers of the Hebrew Bible did not look upon the human species as lost and alone, but rather as comrades of God in a great universal brotherhood.

Among the Greeks we find many portraits of human nature and destiny. It would not be true to say that the Greeks were smiling optimists and unthinking Utopians, nor can a simple generalization be made about the Hellenistic view of the human adventure. At times man is regarded as the plaything of the Olympian deities, and Homer is certainly filled with epic stories of the comedies and tragedies that take place upon earth as a result of the squabbles and quarrels between Zeus and other gods. In general, however, I would say that the Greeks, although they often maintained a tragic view of man, invested that tragedy with a halo of dignity and courage. Man is a tragic figure, pursued by the Furies, always subject to the decrees of Fate, and yet his story remains the most important event upon the surface of the globe. It is not, as in so much modern literature, a mere footnote in the textbook of calamity and catastrophe.

Many are the varying motifs that were played by the Greek minds upon the soft wax of life. The Greeks were terribly afraid of pride and regarded arrogance as among the most unforgivable of sins. That is why they stress the necessity of the Golden Mean: "Nothing in excess." They believed that men and women are under the dominion of Moira, a fate, and that a great deal of suffering is inevitable in the human journey. We must learn, they said, to make friends with pain. We must strive to achieve a manly endurance and we must be very careful not to exceed our human limits "and strive to become like Zeus." They understand, those ancient Greeks, that whatever is human is insecure, that life at best is precarious and that death is man's beloved refuge.

There were pessimists and atheists among the Greeks, men like Theognis who proclaimed "best of all for mortals were it never to have been born, nor to have seen the rays of the burning sun" or like Antiphon, the Sophist, who looked upon life as a brief turn of sentry duty in which every moment of life has its birth and every day begins a new doom. Marriage, to him, was a gamble, at best, a sorrow, a giving of hostages to fortune. If there are children, all is anxiety, and old age has its special burdens. Antiphon is, as Professor W. C. Green of Harvard points out, a spiritual brother of Hamlet, and of the philosopher Hobbes, who found the life of natural man "solitary, poor, nasty, brutish, and short," and a "war of every man against every man." We might add that Antiphon is a spiritual ancestor of the existentialist and of the contemporary defeatist about man and man's hope in the world.

Not only pessimism but atheism goes back tens of centuries ago to such a thinker as Critias, a kinsman of Plato and a friend of Socrates. In a fragment of his which has come down to us, we find his very remarkable interpretation of how law and religion originate. He maintains that men imposed law as re-

straint upon the natural arrogance and sinfulness of human nature. Now, these laws checked open deeds of violence but not
secret ones. "So a clever man invented the fear of the God to
quell wicked and secret offenses, saying that there is a Spirit,
immortal, all-seeing, all-hearing, all-knowing, whom none can
evade." This, the ancient author maintained, is a pleasant deceit
which has no basis in reality. Religion, in other words, is a pious
fraud. The whole theory of modern atheism about religion's being the opiate of the masses, the necessary imprisonment of human impulses, the sanction of morality without which there
would be total chaos among men and nations—this approach to
life has its prototype in the Greek thinker, Critias. This, however, is but part of the Greek story and perhaps the smaller part.

Suffering is here on this earth, but man can come to regard
suffering as educative—a disciplinary process. It is man alone of
all the creatures on earth who has the capacity to respond to the
world, to react affirmatively and creatively with dignity and for-
titude. As it has very beautifully been put, "an oyster secretes a
pearl when irritated by grains of sand," so man, wounded and
irritated by the grains of suffering, secretes many pearls of wisdom and beauty and nobility. It is possible to face misfortune
with heroism and with an unbroken spirit. This it is which the
great Greek dramatists, Sophocles and Aeschylus and Euripides,
all proclaim in one form or another. They affirm the strength of
the human will and the blessing given to man to learn through
his suffering how to transcend it and to rise above it.

These great dramatists saw life steadily and saw it whole.
They did not blink their eyes at the tragic realities of the world,
the cruelties, the passion, the lust which make men often the
helpless plaything of their own emotions.

Memorable and immortal are the portraits of human character that come from this gallery of the Greek dramatists. In the great drama of Euripides, *Hippolytus,* we see before us a young prince, self-centered and very pure and very chaste, a man who rejects the proffered love of his stepmother, Phaedra. Hippolytus is a young man incapable, apparently, of normal human reactions, an escapist from human involvement. The woman in the drama is portrayed as a pathetic and poignant creature, subject to her passions and her roaming thoughts, who by temperament does not have the detachment and moderation of the young prince. Both characters are led to ruin by the faults of their own natures, the prince by his cold self-righteousness. "The nobility of soul has been thy ruin." Phaedra is ruined by her uncontrolled and uncontrollable passionate nature. She is warmhearted and capable of violent emotions, while the young prince is like a cut flower living in prim solitude in some conservatory of chastity.

The Greek dramatist in telling this story wants to point out the heartbreak involved in human life when men and women allow themselves to be swept away on the gusts of emotion or, on the other hand, permit their human and compassionate feelings to be frozen and congealed by a premature and an unjustified self-righteous feeling of emotional superiority.

In another great drama, *Electra,* Euripides portrays the frustrated mother who takes out her anger in life upon her helpless daughter. This is in the story of Clytemnestra—the false wife who found no joy in her new life with her paramour, a woman eternally jealous, who wants to vent her spite upon her daughter Electra, dealing with her as a slave, treating her as the eternally unwedded, a daughter who, in turn, starved of normal happiness, waits patiently for years for her hour of vengeance to come, when she can deal with her mother as her mother has dealt with her.

Here is a picture, dark and gloomy, of the false relatedness be﹅ tween mother and daughter, a story told and retold at least a billion times in the course of history, not only between mother and daughter but between father and son, between husband and wife, the story of frustration, aggression, vengeance, destruction.

But even these dark portraits of the Greek playwright do not tell the complete story of the Greek view of human nature and of human destiny. We find, in the superb and matchless play of Sophocles called *Oedipus Rex,* the story of a great and noble man who is deceived by life, who is caught up in a network of deception and illusion. The central character in this drama kills his father, not knowing that the old man is his father, and marries his mother, not knowing that the object of his affection is his mother, because he, the hero, had been sent far away as a child, as a result of a dire prophecy which the King and Queen had heard upon the birth of this boy baby. But life, playing its cruel tricks, brings Oedipus into the orbit of the parental environment, not knowing that they are his flesh and his blood; when he learns the truth, Oedipus plucks out his own eyes, blinding himself that he may not look upon the light of the sun any more. This is tragedy, but it is also tragedy redeemed by the magnificent heroism with which the hero—disciplined by suffering, ennobled by pain—meets his fate and rises to the stature of true greatness. It is a drama that tells the story which is to be repeated again and again, as we shall find out, of life as a mixture of illusions and of reality. And yet it is perhaps the greatest duty of man to learn how to distinguish between the apparent and the real.

Among the ancient Greeks we find pessimism and atheism, but we also encounter the magnificent story of Prometheus, the heroic view of life of the Stoics, and the thrilling and exalting view of human nature and destiny as taught by Socrates and

Plato. You recall the story of Prometheus—the divine rebel who decided to risk everything in order to save man. First of all he prevented men from foreseeing their death by planting in them "blind hope"—blind because deceptive, since no mortal can live forever; yet in a sense necessary since ordinary men would hardly undertake activity that looks beyond the immediate future if they expected to die forthwith. In other words, Prometheus implanted in man the great gift of hope without which there can be no struggle, no quest, no achievement. Prometheus not only gave hope to man, but also stole fire for man—fire, which is the servant of the human race as well as its potential destroyer. In spite of all the human torments which Zeus imposed upon the rebel, Prometheus nevertheless symbolizes for the whole human race the possibility of our using the blessings of anticipation and partisanship, of hope and of fire, as the blessed servants of human victory.

It is not only in the story of Prometheus but in the whole philosophy of the Stoics that we find the Greek affirmation of life and of the universe and of man as a part of reason. The world is seen as a rational cosmos, an orderly process. There is a bond of sympathy between all the parts of the universe. Man is rational because his reason is a part of the Divine reason; therefore man must learn to act in harmony with nature, to live in accordance with nature, to attempt not the impossible but the possible, to master his emotions, to expect evil, to resign himself to defeat at times, but also to find peace in resignation and noble self-surrender.

What is our human destiny? We can turn for answers not only to the great playwrights and thinkers of ancient Greece whom we have already mentioned, but perhaps above all others to Socrates and his pupil Plato. In Socrates, the doctrine of humanism is accented for the first time. That ugly searcher and prober of truth who called himself a doctor of the soul proclaimed for all time the ideal of self-mastery and of self-control. He taught his generation in Athens that the purpose of life is to attain not fame, not money, not reputation, but rather the improvement of the inner life, the achievement of character. As Professor Werner Jaeger has pointed out, Socrates anticipated the great German poet Goethe, who asked, "What would be the purpose of all of the wondrous show of suns and planets in the universe if it did not make possible the happiness of one human being?" Socrates did not care about the starry pathways and the secrets of matter. He cared only about the welfare of the human being; and he believed that that welfare could be attained only if men searched themselves, if they conquered their youthful passions and their tempestuous lusts, if they came to recognize that vice is only ignorance, and virtue is knowledge, and that if a person really studied his life situation, he would not come to sin willingly. Furthermore, Socrates was the first great Greek apostle of human relatedness. He never tired of teaching his disciples that men cannot exist in isolation from their fellow men, that we are bound together almost organically just as the hand and the foot and other parts of the human body are bound together one with the other. No human organ can exist alone and live, and no man can exist alone, spiritually, ethically, morally, and live.

Now, as we all know, Socrates received the payment that society often gives as its coin of contempt. He was forced to drink the poison hemlock. His supreme disciple Plato must have been shaken to the very foundations of his spirit at the martyrdom of Socrates. Plato, however, felt that it was his task to carry the torch which had been handed to him by Socrates: the quest for truth and justice. Plato saw all the evils done under the sun and recognized man's baseness and society's cruelties and injustices. It could not be otherwise. How could he suffer from illusion about human nature when he saw what had happened to his beloved teacher? He gave immortality to his teacher in the dialogues where he makes Socrates examine the human story and tries to find a thread of meaning in all of its tangled web.

Now, the insights of Plato are among the greatest ever attained by mortal man. We can mention but a few of them in this kaleidoscopic picture of human destiny as seen by the giants of other times. One basic thesis of the greatest Greek philosopher is that man is a reasoning creature in one part of his nature, that he is distinguished from all other beings on earth by the light of his intellect, and that if men would but stop to reflect, they would recognize that reason is the ultimate judge and standard of all values. Sometimes a person says that he is not interested in weighing good against evil or in taking the rational course, that he wants to find his pleasure where he may. Socrates, as given to us by Plato in one of the dialogues, dissects this point of view and proves that even in the realm of pleasure we have to exercise our reason and to try to weigh a present joy against a future pain. He proves, in other words, that an act of immorality, for example, which brings greater trouble in the long run in physical disease or in psychic unhappiness or in emotional guilt feelings, is an error in reasoning and in judgment; for if we human beings would learn the true art of measurement, we would learn to renounce the short-term pleasure for the long-term peace of mind. Here, too, Plato strikes the motif which we find as the guiding theme in our discussion of human destiny: the necessity of distinguishing between appearance and reality—the appearance of pleasure which is deceptive and illusory, and the reality of life-long pain as a result of indulgence and weakness. "To give way to a smaller temporary pleasure is really a weakness of reason."

Man is not only a rational creature; he is an emotional creature as well. He needs not only the satisfaction of the intellect but the satisfaction of the heart: the knowledge of love. In the dialogue called the *Symposium*, Plato presented some of the greatest and most amazing insights into human love. He created one of his famous myths about mankind: that once upon a time human beings were spherical in shape. "They had four arms, four legs, and moved about by revolving like wheels, but Zeus, in fear of their strength dissected them in two." This fantasy of Plato tells a great truth: namely, that men are always searching after a wholeness and a relatedness which are impossible to attain in separation from our fellow human beings. Man alone without love is a fragment, a kind of torso, part of a larger statue of reality. We yearn forever to be reunited with that which has been lost, to become once again an integral part of the larger whole. When we love, we yearn not merely to belong to the beloved, but also to create with the lover new patterns of beauty, new progeny of perfections, children of the mind or children of the body.

Socrates saw that many men do not know how to love or how to reason. He understood them very well. He understood the seekers after power who justified selfishness as the only road to happiness and fame. He looked at the teachers of his day and called them "experts in sounds and in words—who have made a career out of adapting themselves." There can be sin in adaptation as well as an error in maladjustment. This truth is often ignored in our age. We have made such a cult out of adaptation. It is good that Plato has reminded us that the appeasers—the compromisers—in society are always those who are well adjusted to the iniquities and the follies of their day, and that it is only the great prophets, the great teachers, the great martyrs, men like Socrates, who prefer creative maladjustment to sterile, soul-searing adjustment.

There is a section in *The Republic* of Plato which is almost unbelievable in its illumination. The philosopher is meditating upon the various types of government—oligarchy, democracy, tyranny, among them—and, in accordance with his own view that the state is always a mirror of what goes on in the individual soul, he portrays human nature for us more realistically than it has ever been portrayed again until the time of Freud. Here, in these last books of *The Republic,* Plato is so concrete and vivid about the various types of men and women to be found in the world that the picture can never be improved upon for the insights it contains about the varieties of human nature. He imagines a young man, the son of a distinguished father who has been interested only in honor, and of a mother interested only in worldly ambition. The boy follows in the footsteps of the mother, abandons the world of reason, and gives himself over to ambition. It is this ambitious man who creates what Plato calls timocracy. His son, in turn, sees that ambition alone is not enough, that it is fruitless and valueless in the eyes of men of power and of wealth, and so this scion of the next generation devotes himself to the hoarding of money. Notice how Plato describes this: "The desirous money-loving part of the soul ascends the throne and becomes its Maharajah, decked with gold tiaras." Ambition gives way to avarice, and a new sultan, namely, Desire, degrades the reasoning part and the fiery honor-loving part of the soul, to be slaves crouching at the foot of his throne. He allows thought to concern itself with nothing except how to get more money, and spirit to admire and honor nothing but wealth and rich men.

Then what happens? Well, greed creates a state which is essentially unstable, and the plainsmen, lean and sunburned, finding themselves fighting in a battle next to these spoiled tycoons of wealth, fat and puffing, grow disgusted with the dominion of the rich, and so the poor and the oppressed rise in revolt against the oligarchy of wealth, and a democracy is created. The democracy of Plato is one more step, however, on the road to degeneration, because it is a state in which there is growing anarchy, everyone arranging his life according to his own desire with the individual triumphant and society itself neglected. Individualism, as Plato sees it, is a disease of the personality, because personality demands social responsibility and social interrelatedness. The mob rules for a while, and then chaos grows to such an extent that a tyrant seizes power and a dictatorship is established. There is fear and trembling in the city and in the state, and suspicion and murder on all sides. The process of degeneration has reached its nadir and its end.

The various forms of government really reflect the various forms of human nature. The timocrat is the man who is filled with ambition, hating the quiet rationality of his father. His son, in turn, thinks that ambition is not satisfying enough and so he prefers to be a moneygrubber; and then, in turn, his son despises greed because devotion to the acquisition of money involves the renunciation of many pleasures and self-indulgences, and so he becomes a "democrat," giving rein to all his impulses, license to all his capricious desires; the son of the democrat, in turn, becomes a despot, and while tyrannizing over his subjects he gives full rein to his lusts, angers, murderous feelings, hates and aggressions, and lives his life completely uninhibited by moral standards and rational hopes.

I say that Plato really was the forerunner of all modern psychology and psychiatry. He, the great prophet of reason, the supreme rationalist, apparently knew by some magic of genius all the subconscious and unconscious factors in man. He realized that there are many types of human being—men in whom reason dominates, and other men in whom ambition dominates, and still other types in whom the desires rule: the desire for wealth, the desire for love, the desire for power. In each man, says Plato, there are revealed through his dreams many of the dark and bestial phases of his essence. There are in every one of us both rational capacity and passionate desires; and in some of us there is chaos where license rather than freedom rules, and where there is no order whatsoever among the many competing drives.

All political science really is founded upon the analysis that is given in *The Republic* of the various types of states and societies and governments. Plato, thousands of years ago, wrote a prognosis of Hitlerism, telling exactly what happens in a tyranny. If this prognosis had been studied and understood, it might have averted enormous sadness for all humanity.

At the same time, Plato gives his conception of what human nature and human destiny ought to be: namely, the control of reason to dominate the subterranean elements in our natures. Our impulses should not be allowed to break loose. They should always be subordinate to the intellect, and then ambition and desire and passion will play their proper harmonious roles in the total healthy economy of the healthy individual. I do not know of any more original portrayal of human nature, or any more amazing revelation of what man is and can become, of how sons do rebel against their fathers, and take a course of action inconsistent with the pathway of reason and of intellect, of how essential it is to subordinate our passionate and impulsive characteristics to the taming and channeling influences of the mind. Only in this fashion can there come a symmetry in the individual soul rather than the melodrama of inner treason and civil chaos. Only in this way can there be happiness and justice both in the mind of the individual and in the state of society.

Now, Plato, that great apostle of reason, understood that men ofttimes suffer from illusion. They do not know what they want or what they ought to want. They are confused by their senses and the heat of their blood. There is the unforgettable myth of the cave, the story of man living his life in the cave of illusion, chained with his back against the opening so that he sees the sunlight of reality only as a shadow upon the wall. Men, all men, living in the world of the senses, think that what they experience with their eyes and their ears and their senses of touch and taste is the true world of actuality. As a matter of fact, it is only a puppet show, and all the scenes thrown upon the walls of the cave by the reflected rays of light that come through the little entrance merely light up the marionettes, the marionettes of objects and of human beings dancing across the illusory landscape. Then, Plato says, by some great act of will and of strength, one of the slaves breaks loose from his chains and stumbles out of the cave up into the outer world, into the true universe of light and of idea, and here he comes face to face with the sun of goodness and of truth. At first he cannot believe what he sees; and then as he begins to adjust himself to reality, to rejoice in the liberation that he experiences, he becomes ambitious and eager to liberate his brothers from their shadow world. He stumbles back again into the darkness of the cave, and his brothers prefer to stone him to death rather than to accept the message of salvation and of redemption that he brings to them. They still believe that their illusions are the truth and that the shadows upon the wall are not puppets and marionettes but the substance of existence.

The upper world is the world of reason, and the cave is the world of unsubstantiated opinion and of ignorance. Plato wants to say that we human beings are caught too often in the world of appearance and impurity, that it is our task to liberate ourselves from the region of darkness and to come out into the true light of understanding, of goodness and of eternal truth.

This, in Plato, is the destiny of man: to rise above the cave of illusion and to come into the beautiful sunlit realm of Idea, to follow the gleam of reason wherever it will take us. What is man? The greatest Greek philosopher said that man at times is a seeker after pleasure, and it is understandable that the human being wants to get rid of painful stimuli. This is what the greatest modern psychoanalysts would say: that every child wants to expel from his organism that which is painful, just as he wants to take in and to absorb that which is pleasant. The little baby really performs but two acts—expulsion and incorporation—and man, as seen by Plato thousands of years ago, also has the task of expelling the evil and of absorbing the good. Now, much of our life is spent tragically, in taking in things that are not worthwhile, in eating the poison of illusion, untruth, of accepting the husks of food that will not satisfy us. What man ought to do is to eliminate the false values of avarice and ignoble ambition, and to absorb the true foods for the mind and the soul: reason and love. What is our human destiny? Plato would say that it is for us to seek as long as we live to be filled with that which is fitting for man, to be filled with knowledge and truth, not with lust and folly, to reject that which poisons our hearts and our social interrelationships, and to digest as long as we live the food of inner beauty, inner justice, inner reason, to let our souls feast upon the sun of goodness and truth.

• •

The most complete view of human nature ever created in literature is probably that found in the dramas of Shakespeare. The Elizabethan poet intuitively understood the human heart and mind, and clothed that understanding in peerless rhyme and meter, an accomplishment not exceeded since his day. Shakespeare is certainly the ageless diagnostician of human ills, human passions, human hopes—diagnostician, although not therapist, in the final sense of the word. His plays are populated by kings and rogues, clowns and madmen, charming lovers, desperate murderers—the whole panoply of men. One might even say that he who reads and comprehends all of Shakespeare has mastered the textbook of the human soul's anatomy and pathology; he knows much, if not all, about the boils that disfigure the soul and the beauties that glorify the conscience. There are the unforgettable love scenes in *Romeo and Juliet,* the tender misunderstandings in *Twelfth Night* and *A Midsummer Night's Dream;* the consuming jealousy in *Othello,* the hatred of tyranny in *Julius Caesar.*

The gamut of human emotions is run in the plays of the immortal bard. Where can one find a more superb description of self-hate and self-rage than in the lines spoken in *Coriolanus:* "Anger's my meat; I sup upon myself, and so shall starve with feeding."

In *Othello* we find there is enough of a grain of morality in Iago's soul so that we may believe his action. Shakespeare humanizes his characters often enough to make them credible. As one of the critics put it, morality and conscience for many are like pebbles in a shoe, small enough to be felt and to make us uncomfortable, but not to make us stop thinking or walking.

The many moods in one man are portrayed in *Richard II* as the King meditates upon his condition in prison:

Thus play I in one person many people,
And none contented: sometimes am I king;
Then treasons make me wish myself a beggar,
And so I am; then crushing penury
Persuades me I was better when a king;
Then I am king'd again: . . .
And straight am nothing.

Shakespeare indicates matchlessly well how at times we play many roles and are often contented in none of them. When we are beggars, spiritually or emotionally speaking, we want to be monarchs again, and when we are monarchs, we yearn for the simplicity of the life we left behind us.

Man's attitude to life and his deep feeling of depression have never been more graphically presented than in *Hamlet:*

O God! O God!
How weary, stale, flat and unprofitable
Seem to me all the uses of this world!
Fie on 't! ah fie! 'tis an unweeded garden,
That goes to seed; things rank and gross in nature
Possess it merely.

How often the world seems to man an unweeded garden in which poisonous roots and branches of hate and violence and injustice grow, while the flowers and the tender, delicate plants of compassion wither away! Again and again every human being who has any sensitivity at all feels in the mood of Hamlet that "The time is out of joint," or that the world is a "goodly" prison, "in which there are many confines, wards, and dungeons."

Life and death are equally well known to Shakespeare. "The

stroke of death is as a lover's pinch, which hurts, and is de-sired." There is mingled pain and pleasure in the thought of our mortality, and it is consoling to reflect, as Shakespeare re-flects at moments, that "after life's fitful fever, he sleeps well; . . . nothing can touch him further," for death promises "a sea-change into something rich and strange." And as we face it, we must face it together and show one another compassion and love and sympathy; and as the poet understood long before the twentieth century with its new insights into the wise manage-ment of grief, "Good my lord . . . you do, surely, bar the door upon your own liberty, if you deny your griefs to your friend." Shakespeare realized that God has given to us "the fruitful river in the eye," our tear ducts to use in moments of grief and sorrow and bereavement, and we must not be ashamed of that grief, but must possess at last the wisdom to realize that all that live must die, passing through nature to eternity.

The great problem of human life in Shakespeare, as it is in Sophocles and in Plato, is the disparity between appearance and reality. Perhaps the greatest drama that Shakespeare wrote on this problem is his immortal *King Lear*.

King Lear has decided to give up his throne and to divide his possessions among his three daughters. The two eldest protest their love for him in words that melt his heart, and he gives them shares of his possessions, and when Cordelia, the youngest and truest of them does not acquiesce in his wish for flattering pro-testations, he banishes her. Later comes his rude awakening. Now that he is stripped of his power, the father learns "how sharper than a serpent's tooth it is to have a thankless child," for his two older daughters, needing him no longer, treat him with arrogance and contempt. What seemed to be love was mere self-interest on their part. The old King stumbles from one household to another, finding welcome nowhere and then is driven out into the wild night, accompanied only by his fool. He lets the lightning singe his white beard and he goes mad. The tempest in the mind is greater than the tempest in outer nature. Eventually Lear realizes how cruel he has been as a monarch. He is now aroused to a feeling of compassion for those more wretched than himself.

The wild storm within his mind and the raging lightning and thunder in the night itself are fit symbols of what happens to man when he is rejected, when his love is spurned and those who should be most grateful to him prove curs of ingratitude. Every human being has a breaking point, and Lear's breaking point comes when he understands the utter rejection of the daughters in whom he has trusted. It is then that he sees that appearance and reality are light-years apart. Everything that constitutes human tragedy is found in this play. Lear learns that when power is taken away and authority is removed, even a king becomes only a poor old man.

He at last embraces his faithful Cordelia, but it is too late. When her vicious sisters and their husbands have destroyed the faithful Cordelia, Lear stumbles in with her beloved body in his arms. His broken voice cries out in agony, "She's gone for ever . . . She's dead as earth. . . . No, no, no life! Why should a dog, a horse, a rat, have life/And thou, no breath at all? Thou'lt come no more,/Never, never, never, never, never!" These last five words have been described as the saddest ten syllables in the language. The King cannot stand to live any longer; his heart breaks, and he is glad to be released from the "rack of this tough world" which now stretches him no longer.

There is vicious arrogance in this play. The two older sisters are symbols of ingratitude and passion, themselves eaten away by their sensual desires. Their fates are indeed miserable. They suffer from the malice which they brought to the life of their father. They themselves experience the horrors and the agony which they imposed upon those whom they betrayed. Yet, as the Shakespearean critics point out, even in this drama of evil, we find the nobility and grandeur of Lear, his sense of tenderness now for the least of his companions, his recognition of his own share of guilt in the suffering of his subjects, the lesson of sympathy that is born out of his own personal suffering. We encounter the devotion of Edgar to the King, the nobility and sweetness and tenderness of Cordelia. We find the great and wise words spoken by Edgar: "Men must endure/Their going hence, even as their coming hither:/Ripeness is all."

Our human destiny is painted by Shakespeare, in this great tragedy, as the experiencing of evil, of ingratitude and of the bedevilment that comes from surrendering to illusion rather than seeking reality in our human relationships. But the very tragedy itself reveals the nobility of man as well as his baseness, the truth and the beauty that cannot be destroyed, or that, even when destroyed, cannot be erased from the memory of later generations. There is corruption, but there is also compassion. There is hate, but there is also honor. There is iniquity, but there is also integrity to redeem the story of man from utter meaninglessness and torture.

Shakespeare does not end on a note of defeatism. In his early tragedies, the appearance was good, but the reality was evil. In his last play, *The Tempest,* we find that Shakespeare reverses his conclusion: it is the evil that is redeemed. There is in all these plays, as Professor Theodore Spencer of Harvard puts it, a rebirth, a return to life, a new awareness of normality. Listen to Miranda's view of man as given in *The Tempest:* "How beauteous mankind is! O brave new world/That has such people in 't!"

Perhaps it is true that the Elizabethan poet looked upon our earth and our experience upon it as "a little life rounded with a sleep." Perhaps we might say that his philosophy is contained in the three words "Ripeness is all." Certainly the poet is a man of enormous understanding and deep sympathy. In play after play, he uncovers the face of evil, terrible evil, and shows us the cruelties that men and women inflict upon each other, as well as the harsh and relentless blows of fate and nature. We do not know why the evil exists. We must resist it wherever we can with all our strength of mind and body. As Gotthard Deutsch put it, "Where we cannot resist, we must endure." At the same time, Shakespeare in all the magic beauty of his poetry makes us see that the universe is one in which there is not only the problem of evil but also the equally insoluble problem of good. The good does not cancel out all the tragedy, but neither does tragedy cancel out the wonder, the majesty, the exaltation and the beauty of the human spirit. Our human journey must teach us to resist, to endure, to transform that which can be transformed, to accept that which must be accepted, and to rejoice above all in the countless blessings laid in our cradles as our birthright, blessings that accompany us even in the midst of the wracking pains of life, even unto the end.

We have now surveyed something of the background of religion, philosophy, and literature. The Hebrew Bible, the Greek thinkers, and the immortal Shakespeare are all united in proclaiming certain inescapable truths about our deeds. No one of the supreme artists of the past ever denied the reality of sorrow, misfortune and suffering; yet they all felt that men and women are great actors in a significant play, some tragic, some comic, but none meaningless and empty.

This is what creates the mood of tragedy, great tragedy: the feeling that the heroes and the heroines are people of stature, that there is something sublime going on. The Greek dramatist did not look upon an Oedipus and an Electra as strutting little fools, pathetic clowns. No, the essence of tragedy is that sublime human nature is tried and tested in the crucible of suffering, and that is why, when we read or witness a great tragedy, our own emotions are purged and we experience the psychic catharsis, an inner purification, as we live through the storm and the stress, the tensions and the triumphs, of the actors in the human poem.

How great is the difference in attitude and moods between an Aeschylus or a Shakespeare on the one hand, and a Sartre, a twentieth-century nihilist, on the other! How great is the difference between a view of man as a Promethean character, a Titan or a child of God, and the modern view of man as a cipher, a zero, a little buffoon walking amidst towering gigantic buildings, a pathetic little Charlie Chaplin tripping over a wire, falling off the curbstone, being crushed in a mob of anonymous nobodies— one nonentity among many.

The human drama was conceived in majestic and noble terms in the Bible. The story of Adam and his descendants even when sinful and rebellious was still significant. The saga of the Greeks from the time of Homer down through Plato and Plato's successors is an inspiring and challenging story of men pitted against fate, fleeing from the Fury, and sometimes triumphing over the Furies. Man in Christian dogma, sinful worm though he is, was also a beloved of the Divine, saved and redeemed by the grace of God. The story of man in Shakespeare certainly is the story of a creature wounded, afflicted, misunderstood, suffering from many illusions, not making the proper distinctions between appearance and reality, but it is also the story of a creature of great

69

dimensions and noble proportions, the proportions symbolized by an Othello, a Hamlet, an Edgar, a Cordelia. What happened to man with the beginning of the modern age? That is the question that we must try to answer for ourselves.

In many ancient and medieval periods and places man appeared as a king; and then somehow with the dawn of modernity the gay ball was over, and with the dawn of science and technology, the costume of man's importance was stripped from him. The monarch's garb was taken off his back. The mask and the scepter were laid aside, and in the light of scientific day, man seems to be revealed not as prince but as pauper, or, if we can change the metaphor, after the Copernican revolution the geometry of man's life was radically changed. The human being became all of a sudden a point instead of the great center, a dot rather than the throne of reality. What great change occurred to bring modern man to his present melancholy state, to the thought of his meaninglessness and aloneness, to the mood of self-contempt reflected in the pessimistic novels and poetry and philosophy of our day? What was it that transformed him thus from king into fool, from sovereign to slave, from prince to pauper?

The real reasons for modern man's predicament, his sense of worthlessness, his despair about his future, his loss of hope, his poignant aloneness—this is to be the theme of the next chapter. Only when we penetrate into the secret recesses of man's hope and his modern martyrdom can we begin to discover new doors of hope for our human destiny. Only when we understand what it is that science is to man, and what technology and modern economics and modern philosophy are, only when we realize how needlessly we go astray and stumble into paths leading to oblivion—yes, to the very abyss of nothingness—only then can

70

we get back onto the right road leading at last to the Promised Land of human fulfillment and human freedom—the highway of human status, worth, dignity and relatedness.

CHAPTER THREE

Modern Man and What He Faces

FOUR REASONS
FOR HIS PREDICAMENT

Modern man is profoundly confused about his status, his destiny and his future. Ancient man also was confused, and our ancestors in the Middle Ages did not escape perplexity and uncertainty; but before the coming of the Reformation and the Renaissance man developed a basic conviction of his values as a child of God. Both Judaism and Christianity have taught the comforting doctrine that this earth was the center of creation and that man was the lord of that creation. Now all that has been changed in the last few centuries and the human species feels itself lost in vast time and endless space, no longer a child of God but rather a cousin of the chimpanzee, as perishable as a glowworm in a summer night.

No doubt about it, the world today is confused and man experiences many predicaments—moral, spiritual, intellectual. It is very difficult to know to whom to turn for answers in our time. The problems of men are not merely jobs, economic security, competitive power, international peace. There are deeper problems that disturb and split the soul—queries about man's position in life and his haunting feeling of "otherhood" instead of brotherhood. The truth of the matter is that today we do not have a universal language in which to understand one another.

The universes of discourse are more numerous than the planets in space, and, like stars and suns out of their orbits, they are colliding and clashing violently today. Conservative and radical economists disagree with one another about the possibility of future prosperity or depression. Philosophers murder one another verbally in the technical journals of opinion; psychologists and psychiatrists disagree with each other brutally and violently about the basic premises of human nature. There is an infinite variety of moods and approaches today in almost every realm of thought. On the one hand, for example, you find logical positivists, suspicious and scornful of metaphysics. You find the cohorts of naturalism with their rather pedestrian and prosaic acceptance of things as they are. At the other extreme of the philosophic spectrum you find the dark followers of Kierkegaard and those cultists among the intellectuals who worship at the shrine of Sartre and existentialism—the new romantics seeking a thrill, a meaning, a purpose, a rationale out of the pyrotechnics of despair.

Among the thinkers of our time there are those who exalt reason and those who hate it, those who glorify force and those who despise it, those who see all of life reflected in the mirror of sex or economics or the quest for power. These are some of the confusing flora and fauna in the forest of liberalism and the jungle of Marxist weeds. There is no lingua franca today. It is as though we modern men and women were on a vast battlefield with all lines of communication cut and each little unit setting itself up as the high command. Or, to change the metaphor, we men and women today are wandering in a sort of intellectual London fog where no one really can discern who is his foe and who is his friend. The frightening dark is upon us and our words seem hollow even to our own ears.

Modern man is in a terrible predicament intellectually because there is so little agreement as to the basic meaning of existence. The quarrels that divide scientists, psychiatrists and philosophers from one another also reveal themselves in religion, where you will find humanists and supernaturalists and orthodox theologians offering salvation in a thousand different cups with the wine of life having a different tang in each cup.

Not that we should lose our sense of perspective and feel that this is something entirely new in human experience. Man has had his battles of the spirit in many a century before our own. A basic difference, however, is that there was in previous ages the cement of dogma which bound society together. The fabric of life then was made up of the silken threads of belief and faith and doctrine which finally became "the long stakes and the strong ropes that kept the tent of life bound to the earth of reality." You and I know today how many intellectuals experience a nostalgia, for example, for the Middle Ages. That is one of the reasons for so much conversion to orthodox Christianity among the uprooted and bewildered, the homeless thinkers and poets, the unhappy writers of our time. Oh, for the sanity and security of a St. Thomas Aquinas, they cry out—oh, for the beautiful simplicity of a Francis of Assisi!

It is not only among the Christians that there is this yearning for a return to the medieval synthesis. Jews also are part of this fragmentized universe. They grow tired at times as they listen to the din of the confused counsel and the heated partisanship, the feverish frenzy and the sterile debate, that are compounded out of Jewish fear and frustration, and they experience at times a deep yearning to return home to some simpler Jewish epoch, to find the way back to the certainties that have been exploded away by all the TNT of modernity.

Jews in other ages were, of course, not untouched by the

struggle for philosophic adjustment and the attainment of intellectual "respectability." The whole of medieval Jewish philosophy in a sense was an unnatural phenomenon, a form of display, a desire to be at home in the parlor of Aristotle and the agora of Plato—like a rather plain and simple woman who feels compelled to deck herself out in the jewels of her more elaborately dressed neighbors and rivals—so the Jewish philosophers of the Middle Ages wore borrowed garments over the simple dress of Biblical and Rabbinic Judaism. In other words, it is not only our age of Jewish thought which wishes to feel at home in the speculations of Dewey and the discoveries of Freud; Maimonides and Crescas are ancestors of that mood, and Philo was its spiritual grandfather. Assimilation on the part of Judaism to foreign ideologies is no recent innovation.

This is all parenthetical and digressive as far as our main problem is concerned—namely, the predicament of modern man. I have maintained so far that that predicament is born out of the tremendous confusion in our age, the uncertainty and the unclarity about what we human beings are and what we should be, what we can hope for and what we can achieve.

Before I attempt to analyze the reasons for our present predicament, I would like to characterize the age in which we live. Ours is a power age born out of the Protestant approach rooted in Calvinism, which makes aggression legitimate in many areas and sensual pleasure illegitimate—a supreme taboo creating, therefore, the typical "basic personality" of our Western culture, with success, not salvation, as the goal of life and erotic indulgence as the Circe of doom . . . faster, richer, more, more . . . the comparative degree is the honorary degree of our culture and our culture is threatened with catastrophe—the blast and bang of splitting atoms and super-rockets.

The majority of men haven't the time or the patience or the training to reflect upon their real predicament, but the intellectuals are more and more articulate about the tragic plight of our time. Man is a problem to himself, haunted by a sense of hopelessness, and has been so for the last several centuries. Modern poetry, art, religion, philosophy, brood upon the cosmic eviction papers that have been served by the sheriff from the scientist's laboratory. Man has been put out, bag and baggage, from his cozy mansion of the universe, and he has been set down on the cold curbstone of reality. During these past several hundred years many men have been looking for some high court before which they could plead their case. They yearn to be given a consoling and sheltering dwelling place once more, a Divine home, but in court after court the judge has charged the jury, "Bring in the verdict, guilty." The judges have been hard and granite-like men, cool and detached men, physicists and astronomers and chemists, unemotional men . . . Bruno, Kepler, Darwin, Freud.

Science and philosophy, as we shall see, have joined hands with economics and psychology to evict man from the center of the universe, and make him a relatively unimportant inhabitant of a small island of stardust wandering in empty space. Modern man in one mode or another howls out his elegy of aloneness, echoing the words of Shakespeare, "I have no brother, I am like no brother; . . . I am myself alone."

I am myself alone—these are key words that appear again and again in the lines of the poets of our times, the imagery of our novelists, the grotesque figures of our impressionist and surrealist painters. Man evicted from the House of Value—this displaced person living in the squatter's camp of meaninglessness is you and myself, according to the testimony given on the witness stand of truth by the experts of modernity.

And who are these experts, and what do they teach? In the first place modern scientists conspired unconsciously to deflate man, to make him unimportant, almost irrelevant. You recall that before the time of Copernicus, the human species was certainly regarded as the beloved of God. Then the revolution occurred in astronomy. Instead of the earth's being the center of the world, it was mere matter, one planet among others revolving around the sun. Man began to be terribly frightened about this scientific revolution. It was out of hysteria and panic and fear that religion battled the new astronomy, and out of deep unconscious awareness of the impact that these discoveries through the telescope would have upon man's self-esteem.

The balloon of human pride began to collapse then under the pinpricks of astronomy, biology and psychology. Man, who had thought himself terribly important, began to feel terribly unimportant when he saw first of all how small and minor the whole earth was in the realm of infinite space, and then he felt even smaller as he came to recognize through the eyes of Darwin that the whole human species was just a little more advanced protoplasm, a more complex relative of the animal world. Freud in a certain sense brought about the climax of ego deflation. One blow after another fell upon man's sense of his own importance, and he began to cower under these blows. Instead of feeling that he was a valuable creature, he began to think of himself as a piece of cinder, a higher form of ape, a creature of fleeting reason gifted with a little more intelligence than the occupant of a jungle tree, but that is all. It is hard to accept with equanimity these blows to our human vanity; and for these last three centuries we have been battling against these ego-deflating theories, sensing our defeat in advance. Well, humanity has now made an uneasy peace with science. It has come to believe that the world is not the center of creation, that man is the product of long evolution and is indeed a relative of the ameba and the monkey and that our minds are like occasional headlights gleaming in the darkness of the unconscious and the subconscious. This acceptance, however, does not make us happy. Man has realized somewhere in his nature that he has lost his hope. The bank of science has, as it were, foreclosed the mortgage on his dwelling of dignity: the mortgage of modern discoveries in astronomy, physics, chemistry, biology and psychology that has been excessively burdensome and we have not yet learned how to redeem the mortgage. Science has helped to put man out on the street with his tattered religious furniture and his age-old spiritual tapestries, and the comfortable rocking chairs of human hope and human pride, and there he has been sitting out on the street, the cold, dark street of scientific reality, for the last three centuries. No wonder that man has come to feel himself a frightened, deserted, alienated personality, a creature of chance without a roof of cosmic respectability over his head and with no walls of meaning to shelter him from the stormy blasts of icy cynicism, pessimism, fatalism.

It is not science only that is responsible for modern man's predicament. There is a second reason for our state of confusion, and that lies in the field of philosophy itself. When modern science began its demolition of the scaffolding of medieval thought, and when the rush of new discoveries unsettled man and his cozy certainties about life and the world, there began to be new theories gestating and fermenting—theories about man, his mind, his knowledge, his relationship to other human beings and to nature itself.

For a long time people took more or less for granted, in a

kind of naïve commonsense fashion, that the colors and the sounds in the objects of nature existed where they seemed to exist. But then with the work of Galileo and Sir Isaac Newton, and the theory which developed that all that actually existed was matter moving in space, there developed a number of philosophical ideas very radical and revolutionary in their impact and influence. Among them was the theory that it is the human mind that somehow splashes the world with color and sound, that these qualities do not exist in outer realities but are mere subjective projections of the human intellect. The name of John Locke, one of the great names of modern thought, is associated with this doctrine, and this trend continued in the work of Bishop Berkeley and David Hume—men who came to tear down all the commonsense beliefs of the previous centuries asserting that we can never prove that anything exists outside of our minds, that as far as we are concerned when we do not see and perceive and know something, it is nonexistent, and that as a matter of fact there is no possibility of proving either the existence of any object in nature or of a persisting mind in ourselves. All that we human beings experience are streams of sensation, a color here, a sound there, a form someplace else, fragmentary data that we string together with the beads of our habits.

Philosophy began to perplex and confuse man by undermining all his lifelong certainties, like termites eating away at the foundations of a great house until the walls themselves collapse. Philosophy began to make man doubt both matter and mind. We see this trend, for example, in the theory of John Locke that a human being is just a mental substance without any real relationships to other mental substances or persons. We are little atoms, independent individuals, and we project all the colors onto the canvas of nature. They are not really there. Not only do we project our emotions onto the canvas of society. Everything is really only an appearance, a kind of puppet show. Man is a lonely, private, isolated individual, according to Locke. While this concept made possible revolutions in politics and economics, giving new strength to the trend toward individualism and freedom and personal rights, as a doctrine it is very subversive of human relatedness and of an organic connection in society. If every person is a private, isolated mental substance, where, then, are the bridges between men and women? They have been dynamited away by a radical subjectivism. This theory, as Professor F.S.C. Northrop of Yale has pointed out, leads directly to madness and eccentricity in painting and sculpture, to total self-centeredness and selfishness and hedonism in ethics, and to extreme laissez-faire theory in economics.

Man becomes isolated, divorced from his social context. Thinkers begin to argue very seriously in defense of what is known as solipsism—the belief that the individual alone exists and his mind alone is real; that everything that occurs is mere appearance. I know that this sounds mad, and yet it is one of the great theories in modern philosophy—the ultimate end of the road as far as human aloneness is concerned. Bishop Berkeley in one form, and his successors since his day in other forms, have proclaimed the impossibility of disproving this belief that I and I alone exist, and that everything I think I see is just a product of my waking dream. You call it absurd, laughable, mad—apply whatever adjectives you wish. Nevertheless, this is part of the world mood of the last three centuries, this extreme individualism and subjectivism. Man has felt himself unrelated to anything, to God, to nature, to other human beings. The philosopher Leibnitz spoke of human beings as "windowless monads." The German philosopher Fichte in the year 1800 wrote as follows: "I shall stand absolutely independent . . . the product of my own will. . . . I am wholly of my own creation. . . ."

You can trace the influence of this theory of solipsism and individualism all through the eighteenth and nineteenth and twentieth centuries. Scientists like Eddington and Jeans made popular the belief that all that really exists is the human mind and that what we regard as matter and objects in nature are merely products of our creative intellects. In other words, "It is thinking that makes everything so." This is individualism gone rampant, but it is the characteristic mood of the modern world; man has been told that he is alone and that he is isolated from all other substances, that there are no real bridges between himself and the world except as he creates them out of his own imagination; and man has embraced this lonely destiny and made a virtue out of his tragic defeat. "All right," he has said to himself, "if I am a lonely atom, and all my relationships with fellow human beings and with the great world of matter are mere illusion, subjective appearance, then I will exalt myself and I will glorify my power as the builder and the destroyer of worlds."

This is what happened actually in the philosophy of Immanuel Kant—the most powerful and revolutionary philosopher, perhaps, of modern times. He in his thinking embraced this lonely, unrelated, isolated conclusion of science; but instead of saying that man is a worm, a nonentity, a zero, Kant went to the other extreme and said, "Although we can never understand ultimate reality and we can never peer behind the curtain that separates us from the Absolute, nevertheless everything that we do see in the world is a projection and a creation of the human mind. I, the thinker, am the most important being in all reality, and the categories of my understanding determine whatever

81

truth and knowledge can be obtained on this earth." In other words, modern philosophy has oscillated and vacillated between two extremes, but always in the orbit of individualism and alienation. One philosophic mood has been that of total deflation of man—the spoiled darling of God dethroned and sent into exile, and therefore, a meaningless wanderer upon the face of reality. A first reaction to this eviction of man from the throne room of creation by the scientists was despair, discouragement, and total deflation; then as modern man began to assimilate his new doctrine by a process of reaction formation, he began to weave for himself new princely garments out of the threads of his own intellectual and mental power and pride. He said in effect, "All right, I am no longer the child of God, but I am my own creator, and the whole world is merely the product of my sovereign intellect. What I see makes the world live, and when I shut my eyes there is no world; when I shut my ears there are no sounds. Everything depends upon me—the lonely creator of meaning and of knowledge. I am myself alone—but what an 'I' this little ego of mine turns out to be—all-powerful, all-important, all-creative."

Success, power, work, prestige—these become the key words in modern man's striving and life goal. Part of this emphasis comes from the desperation of humanity when it feels that it is no longer the center of the universe, that its soul has been dissolved and its whole human importance deflated. Man needs to believe in his own value; and if he can't believe in it as a child of God, then he will believe in his value as a producer of goods, an accumulator of tangible, glowing gold and silver and platinum, of territory and factories. No wonder that modern man has become a worshiper at the shrine of science, science that has opened new doors to mastery of nature. He needs this mastery in order to drown out the sounds of his own helplessness, the feeling of his worthlessness as a result of the new view of the universe and of himself as a bit of unimportant stardust, a cinder in the eye of God. Science becomes for him an instrument and a tool for power and progress and success to replace the old dream of personal salvation. Money is valued as the means to bigness by which man can hide from himself his own spiritual nakedness and emptiness. If you are a success, you don't have to have contempt for your own being, and so you become tied to the transmission belt of work, work, more work, power, more power. You give up the ideal of home and family. You come to regard all pleasure and sex as evil, a part of the sinful distractions from the workbench which alone can confer dignity upon your little day on earth.

There is a profound economic reason for modern man's predicament—the machine age and the technological revolution, in which a relatively few gain enormous power, and the majority become merely parts of an impersonal machine. The automated factory system swallows up all the personal human values that gave beauty and significance to the human adventure in simpler and more poverty-stricken eras. Look at the world today. We see it as an impersonal machine. Man has been changed into a function, an adjunct to a tool, a manipulator of a bolt, in a great beehive of gadgets of steel and iron. The human person disappears in the vast collective enterprise of an earth that is turned into a factory. The average individual becomes not a person but a focus, an intersection point of differing tasks. Man is an intersection of economic and financial tracks. More and more the human being feels himself an automaton—a slave to the machine, an adjunct to the running belt, a dropper of lubricating oil in the production line. Modern economics makes man feel enormously deflated and dependent, and dependent now not upon a good and predictable mother or father, but on an Impersonal Ghost, the ghost of world economy—the frightening ogre of the unknown. Man, once the child of God, has become the martyr to the machine, the expendable appendage to the impersonal assembly line.

We have seen the scientific, the philosophic, the religious and economic sources of human alienation in the modern world. More and more man has estranged himself from status and significance. He could sue science and philosophy for alienation of affection—the alienation of Divine Love and human interdependence. Man has become a cog in a great mechanism, the world of the factory and the marketplace.

The great philosopher Nietzsche once said, "Woe to him who hath no home." Similarly, we can say woe to modern man, because he has felt himself driven out of a cozy, comfortable, consoling home, the home of the Middle Ages and of antiquity, a home where he was the beloved son, the chosen favorite of the universe, adorned with the coat of many colors. Modern science and philosophy have stripped man of his coat of many colors and driven him out of the eternal dwelling place. He is indeed a displaced person, this modern worker and citizen. He lives in a society which is more and more impersonal, which is more and more concerned with profits and production. He knows himself to be a mere link in a long and infinite chain, the assembly line of the universal factory. If he is not caught as a cog in the machine, he feels himself to be a manipulator of machines or of other men. Things and people are objects to be used, twisted, exploited, not primarily to be understood, loved or appreciated, for this is part of the mood of our mechanistic and hardheaded civilization. True, there has been from time to time a romantic revolt against the realism of the scientific countryside. Poets like

Byron and geniuses like Goethe, artists like Picasso—each one in his own way has rebelled against the emptiness of the landscape or the mechanism of the human scene. The whole Romantic movement has been a kind of spiritual protest against the fragmentation of the human spirit. The protest is reflected in this superb passage from the German poet Hölderlin: "You see craftsmen but no men, thinkers but no men. Does this not resemble a field of battle where hands and arms and all the limbs are strewn about in fragments, while the shed blood of life soaks into the sand?" Yes, this poetic image is terribly and tragically descriptive of the condition in which we find ourselves.

Our world is a battlefield and we modern men are legs and arms and separate organs, symbolic of the partial engagement of human energy in the daily task. The whole man is not required any longer for the work of the day. It is just a person's hands or his feet or some specialized skill which becomes routine after a while—this is what makes humanity in this era of specialization and division of labor so inwardly miserable.

No wonder that we look in vain in our literature and in our hearts for a sense of inner coherence in the human story. No wonder that man feels terribly forsaken. Everywhere one turns, one finds exploded ideologies and blasted faiths. Marxism made it seem very clear that most of the ideologies by which man has lived in the past appear to be rationalizations of his economic status. Freud has made us quite aware of the capacity of rationalization to cover up the real reason for our deeds and our thoughts. We are suspicious of ourselves and our neighbors. We have no sense of organic unity. We feel a deep anguish, and out of that anguish and our sense of isolation we are drawn into some kind of extremist group, religious, philosophical, or political.

The sources of modern man's predicament are many. Science took away from him his status as a favorite child of God. Philosophy cut the lines of communication between man and nature and made the individual both supreme and at the same time extremely isolated; economics, built on the Protestant theory of work and thrift as the means of Divine Grace, has fashioned a factory civilization in which millions of men become anonymous nonentities lost among the machines whose appendages they have become. All in all, these are sufficient explanations of modern misery.

There is, however, another and deeper reason, or I might say a more personal reason, for contemporary confusion and feelings of lostness and aloneness. This is the psychology factor which, granting provocative external circumstances, will lead man to a congealing sense of his unrelatedness.

A child begins his life story with twin yearnings: to absorb and swallow the pleasant, and to reject and expel the unpleasant. He identifies with his mother, whom he sees as an omnipotent, powerful figure from whom he derives not only his supply of milk but also his very important supply of self-esteem. In a certain sense man begins life, then, with an attitude to other human beings—to those who are closest to him—not so much selfish as highly self-centered in nature. The baby looks upon the adult in his environment, particularly the mother, as an instrument for satisfying his own crying subjective needs. Some human beings never outgrow this early subjectivism, this clinging to the object and this using of the object as a means to one's own end. One might even maintain that we begin our lives by using people, not loving them. Early in our development there comes a threat from one source or another of the loss of love and the loss of protection. The child looks for milk and there is none. The

86

child cries for attention and the room is empty. A loss of help and protection means a loss of self-esteem. An ego that is loved feels strong. A deserted one feels weak, exposed to danger. Here is a birth of anxiety and aloneness. The child very early in his human journey knows whether he is protected or deserted, loved or rejected, and out of these first experiments in interpersonal relationships he weaves the warp and the woof of his life fabric.

Our involvement with our fathers and mothers is so enormously close, and sometimes seems so dangerous, that we try to withdraw, to put a wall or barrier between ourselves and those who are closest to us in flesh and blood. We are afraid of our feelings for them or of their feelings for us. We feel guilty or ashamed or anxious, and so sometimes we create a cold, unemotional attitude as our defense against our undesired and frightening feelings.

Many a philosopher who proclaims the doctrine of solipsism may really have accepted this system of total aloneness in order to escape a possible Oedipal conflict. He does not have to worry about his feeling for his mother or for any other woman, nor about his attitude toward his father or any other man, since he has now removed all human and natural objects from reality and has proclaimed them merely to be the creations of his own omnipotent mind. Many a subjective idealist and many a cold rational scientist afraid of emotion might be well understood as a terrified and frightened infant, isolating himself from his emotions toward his father and his mother.

Psychiatry knows, for example, of many phobias and anxieties that make people afraid to go into the street alone. The truth often is that the individual is not afraid of the street, but rather is afraid of his own isolation. He feels isolated partly because he has been afraid of warm human contacts and the instinctual excitement aroused in him by nearness to other human beings. Remember also that often the neurotic who is obsessed with the thought of his isolation is really expressing an even more primitive reality, namely, the lack of narcissistic supplies, the withdrawal of the mother, of the milk of love. A person can create a beautiful philosophy, a magnificent poem, a great novel, crying desolately about man's cosmic aloneness, when as a matter of fact it is merely a later description of a real childhood wound—rejection or desertion or disapproval by the parental figure.

The fear of death, which is also connected with the thought of aloneness, and which is so predominant in the writings of Kierkegaard and Heidegger and Sartre—this rather morbid preoccupation with annihilation and death—can also be traced back psychologically to the child's dread of being left alone. Death is the ultimate loss of love, and annihilation the ultimate form of vengeance—the disappearance of a person seems sometimes to be merely the fulfillment of a hostile and aggressive wish, of some feeling of rage which has never quite been articulated in speech. Fear of the dark is also reducible to the fear of being alone. Freud quotes the child who is afraid of the dark as saying, "If someone talks, it gets lighter." This is a beautiful and memorable way of expressing the human longing for comradeship. At the same time, as we develop psychologically, we not only yearn for companionship, we are afraid of it. We are afraid of the emotions, the desires, the impulses that will be aroused in us by close contact with others, and so sometimes we make a virtue out of our isolation and unrelatedness; we think that we have thus escaped all the consequences of our erotic instincts and aggressive desires. If we can convince ourselves that we exist alone, independent, private and are our own complete masters,

as Berkeley and Hume and other thinkers of their day proclaimed—if this is possible to believe and to assert—then we
have condemned ourselves to a kind of solitary emotional imprisonment. But we have also warded off many terrible and
frightening dangers that seem like ghosts and ogres coming from
childhood experiences. There are some people who want desperately to be alone because they suspect that they cannot manage
their inner feelings in the presence of other men and women.
They have no confidence in their power to control their murderous, lustful, destructive desires; out of such psychic factors
many a philosophy of idealism has been fashioned.

On the other hand, we know that multitudes of men and
women dread aloneness more than anything else. From their
earliest days on earth, they look for signs of affection and protection and grow hysterical when the benevolent parent closes
the door and withdraws. Many of us at times are afraid of being
left as foundlings upon the doorstep of the universe, abandoned
by father, mother and God. We need to reassure ourselves constantly that we are valued and valuable creatures, and we suffer
terrible heartbreak when we come to the conclusion that there is
no one who cares for us, and that this is a universe ultimately
uncared for by any providential guiding hand. That is one reason why multitudes cannot stand the thought of atheism: it re-
awakens within them the feelings of abandonment by earthly
father and earthly mother.

Many, of course, are the varying temperaments among men
and women, and there are psychological factors at work in every
philosophy and in every art. A stoic may well be seen as a person who rejoices in throwing off dependence upon anyone else,
in liberating himself from human needs. He stands alone, de-
fiant, unprotected, and proud.

Modern man's philosophic and literary creation can be understood best only if we have certain psychological instruments at our command. One type of person cannot tolerate uncertainty and doubt: he is obsessed with the need for finding some absolute truth, some perfect system, some intellectual haven of rest. An individual of this type may indeed fling himself into the arms of a traditional church in order to escape the haunting unknown. Psychologically he belongs to the type of human being who is terrified about his own instincts and has to have everything clearly defined for him lest he cross any of the forbidden barriers. He needs intellectual certainty in order to give himself emotional assurance against his own wild inner impulses. Sometimes a person creates a philosophy of wonderful nobility and unselfishness in order to fight his own unconscious self-centeredness and anger. Many men and women escape from their emotions into intellectual problems: in such instances, a scientific discovery or a philosophic system is really a disguise for some very primitive and emotional response. A great physicist or chemist may have gone into his probing and restless quest for truth because of an emotional restlessness and uncertainty about the forbidden realm of sex, a realm he did not understand, which was opaque and obscure on account of the dark and foreboding attitudes of parents toward this tabooed subject.

Think of the varying philosophies of life expressed in our age. Here is Bertrand Russell, who asserts his aloneness and the meaninglessness of traditional religion. He exhibits a pride in thought as omnipotent against the world of unfeeling matter. One is illuminated, in thinking about the reasons for Bertrand Russell's personal outlook, when one learns that Russell was an orphan and knew a great deal of rejection and loneliness in his own childhood. He projected that onto the universe, saying in effect, "Since I have been deserted, I say that the whole world outside myself is of little consequence, while I, through my intellect, become potent and powerful, almost omnipotent." The same psychological explanation can be applied to the conflict-laden and psychically tormented childhood of George Santayana, also scarred and wounded terribly by early loneliness—a loneliness that later became sublimated and crystallized into the unforgettable beauty of Santayana's prose poems and his philosophic works.

If Sigmund Freud is right in judging that much of our later intellectual speculation is conditioned and colored by our early patterns of relationship with parents and brothers and sisters, and if it is true, as seems undeniable, that the realm of sex is predominant in determining the color that we are to have in our life fabric, then we can understand more clearly than ever why some people celebrate and rejoice at the thought of aloneness— for it removes them from temptation and emotional conflict— while others are terrified at the thought of being abandoned and deserted and unrelated. We can realize with a new clarity what philosophies of doubt and negation mean. A thinker who says, "I can never make up my mind as to the nature of reality; I am a total agnostic," can have his words translated into emotional equivalence in some such fashion as this: "I do not really know what the relations between my father and mother were, or what my own feelings toward my parents should have been. I can never make up my emotional mind." In other words, such a thinker projects his emotional and psychic doubts onto the universe and creates quite an acceptable and often very complicated theology or metaphysics out of mental instability and uncertainty.

We are well acquainted with thinkers who deny reality, who

look with skeptical and jaundiced eyes upon the outer world, who are eternally the negativists and nihilists—men like Berkeley and Hume and in some respects, Kant. What psychologically was eating them? What is the inner anatomy of their mood of negation and denial? I am sure that many a thinker who has cast aspersions upon external and objective existence really was expressing something far more primitive and childlike in nature. He just could not stand the thought of what Freud called "the primal scene"—the shock and bewilderment that came to the little boy in his first awareness of eroticism in the relationship of his parents. Wishing to repress, deny, wipe out of existence, the ugliness which he attributed to the marital situation of father and mother, he ended by washing away all of reality and declaring that the world of sound and color and form and matter is sheer illusion.

The agnostics and the skeptics of the world seem to be brooding about God and nature and matter; in actuality many of them have never recovered from their initial obsession which was brooding about masculinity and femininity, about love and hate, about the conflict between their passions and their consciences. Those who go beyond skepticism to total negation are men and women who are consoled—strangely enough—by the thought that everything is illusion. For if everything is illusion, then even their emotions, their passions, their angers and their involvements with their first love objects, mother and father, also become unreal, and need no longer to be a matter of concern and of inner torment.

Psychoanalysis makes many things very clear to us that otherwise would be obscure and opaque forever. It is no exaggeration to say that some economists whose whole lives revolve around the realm of production and distribution of goods and of food are, psychologically speaking, expressing their interest in milk and the satisfaction of hunger—the first stage in the development of the human personality. Other writers, poets, and thinkers, who proclaim the doctrine of a good God and cling to this concept of an all-loving father, are revealing their psychological drives toward dependence and eternal approval at the hands of a father figure. The ethical teachers of civilization who subtly analyze standards of right and wrong, good and evil—one might even say the great social reformers in human history—build their great and noble sublimations upon the foundation of a very early and childlike concern with "doing what Mother wants, obeying Father's wishes." Ethical theory is an adult translation of the human being's attempt to create a superego or a conscience out of the prohibitions and the permissions of the parent; when the parental voice is disobeyed or the command is flouted, there sometimes comes a feeling of panic and hysteria, of anxiety and depression.

In multitudes of men and women, these psychological factors are at work continually, whether they appear in painting, sculpture, poetry, philosophy, or just in daily living where we experience a tragic sense of emptiness, a painful sensation of aloneness, of being unloved and unwanted. The world today conspires to make many people feel unloved and unwanted, and makes many people also feel very guilty about their attitudes toward fellow human beings. Our society realistically and objectively encourages us to use people rather than love them, to treat our human comrades as objects to be exploited in the furtherance of our own goals. No wonder we become anxious about our "milk of love," acceptance and approval. No wonder we are often haunted and tormented by vague feelings of sin and guilt, just because we treat persons as things. We know in our hearts that we should have grown beyond the babyhood attitude toward the world, that is, of regarding human beings as objects to be exploited for their food-giving value. We know that we should have become mature enough to treasure our loved ones for their own sakes rather than as dispensers of mental and psychic vitamins for our nourishment. The truth is that many of us just have never grown mature enough to develop a genuine interest in other human beings on their own terms—to regard them as subjects rather than as objects in the private economy of our needs.

The objective truth of the matter, psychologically speaking, is that, of course, we do not live alone. Our consciences as well as our minds are fashioned by the patterns given to us by mothers and fathers, aunts and uncles. We become aware of ourselves as a matter of fact only by contrasting our unformed egos with the powerful objects around us, giving us laughter, love, suppport and milk. We are never isolated and independent atoms; quite the contrary—we are human electrons always revolving in some larger orbit, some greater content of relatedness.

One of the supreme geniuses of world literature is Dostoevski who in his life and work documented a good deal of what we have been saying concerning modern man's predicament and his psychological confusion and perplexity. "We are all unaccustomed to life," says one of Dostoevski's heroes. The author himself had been a very lonely little boy who grew up in an environment of insecurity with a very antisocial and unsuccessful doctor–father. "A being who becomes accustomed to everything, that I think is the best definition one can give of man." This is one of Dostoevski's comments on human nature. He was enormously frustrated and warped and twisted by his father. Once he said, "I would like to crush the universe. . . . I am alone and so are all men."

Dostoevski lived a very full and paradoxical life. He gained early fame as a writer, then became involved in political struggle and strife and was sentenced to prison and spent years languishing in a Siberian cell surrounded on all sides by the most degraded human types. After he returned from his exile, he began leading a very turbulent existence—falling in love, and finding love both fire and ice; pursued always by some kind of demonic fury, consumed with a passion for gambling, always losing, at the roulette wheel; punishing and torturing himself for some crime which he could not seem to expiate; becoming involved in all kinds of crazy and harebrained schemes; writing his immortal novels; subject more and more to epileptic seizures, relieved by mystical ecstasy during some of his frightening fits—and always somehow pursuing God and seeking for the meaning of life out of personal anxiety and torment; becoming the first great geographer of the human unconscious in the realm of modern literature, a forerunner of Freud and of psychoanalysis.

"God has tortured me all of my life." This phrase that he puts into the mouth of one of his characters expresses his own experience. He never knew a calm and easy, a comfortable, faith. There was always something demonic and passionate in his quest for the Divine, and always Dostoevski was the poet of man's aloneness. He had forever a feeling that he had to defend himself against himself, that man was his own worst enemy, part of him seeking an alliance with Satan, and another part seeking a peace pact with God.

All the novels of Dostoevski are filled with the problems of God and faith and man's hidden nature, and the difference between the surface of experience and the deep waters of suffering and the inner world of passion and impulse. Essentially, the

95

Russian novelist is the great proclaimer of man's aloneness. All throughout his life he was running—running into the embrace of many women's arms, trying to escape from his feeling of desolation and desertion, gambling away his days and his nights and also writing immortal poetry in the form of his novels, seeking a peace that never came to him because he had been warped, twisted, molded and distorted in his childhood and his early youth by a morbid, dark, fear-filled father. All the facets of the modern world—with its vast time and empty space, its lonely individualistic mind, its factory civilization, and its jungle of the subconscious and the unconscious—received the lightning flash of recognition through the pen of the genius of Dostoevski.

His heroes and heroines are often brutal and bestial—murderers and prostitutes—underground men and women. In their lives and in their thoughts we feel the mood of desolation, of alienation, of man's essential estrangement from significance. In a way we can say that the novels of the Russian writer are beautiful expressions of the sadism and the masochism inherent in human life, at least in much of human life. A man revenges himself upon his parents or his brother or his environment by begriming life with the dirt of resentment, the mire of hate. You can smear life artistically, as the painter often smears his canvas, and thus pay it back for childhood frustrations and rage. You can create a philosophy of pessimism in order to subdue other men to your dark outlook, or to express your hostility to life in socially approved form—the death wish cropping out in many novels and in much of philosophy.

It is not only in Dostoevski, it is in many of his followers and imitators, that we find the theme of human hopelessness and despair. This motif is not merely a reflection of economic and social conditions, namely, war, poverty, social oppression. It is also an expression of disguised masochistic moods: "Poor little me, violated and ravished by this violent meaningless universe, deserted and rejected by God, man and society."

This attitude to life reflects itself in the subjectivism of Locke, the idealism of Berkeley, the solipsism of Fichte, the subjectivity of Kierkegaard, and in the writings of Joyce and Kafka and Sartre. To be sophisticated today is to be miserable; to be intellectual is to be forlorn, even gregariously forlorn in some warm cult of mutually cherished feelings of alienation.

Not that there is any surprise in modern man's feeling of alienation and aloneness. His handiwork has conspired to make man an "evictee" from significance, a fugitive from value. Towering skyscrapers and mile-long assembly lines and the vast modern impersonality of our urban civilization all surely justify man in feeling deprived of status and dignity. Today the church and the synagogue have become like the vermiform appendix, mere vestigial remnants in the organism of contemporary culture. What is important today is matter and mastery. A century ago we believed in the escalator of progress. "Progress" now turns out to be a round trip, a circular journey.

I can understand the appeal of this cult of alienation today. It touches upon the masochistic in all of us. It seems to fit the limited facets of our experiences. It lifts us up temporarily to some mountain peak, even if it is the cliff of despair.

Subjectivism is a very seductive doctrine. It flatters the ego, the way that Berkeley and Kant unconsciously flatter the deflated ego of modern man. They said that the mind of the individual is alone existent, important, creative. Well, if the mind of the individual is the creator and the synthesizer of experience, how important it becomes in the scale of values and how irrelevant is the doctrine of man's minuscular value in a universe of infinite space!

Yes, the doctrine of individualism and of man's subjective importance became a protective shield against the howling winds of universal space. It was the warm fireside in the snowstorm of modern science. It proclaimed to man, "You are the center of consciousness. You are the passport-giver to reality. You and you alone stamp the visa for entry into actuality. If you refuse the seal of your mind, then the objective world stands outside the door of your intellect, forever impotent, fuming, hopeless, homeless."

The slick subjectivism of modern philosophy can be understood partly now as a revolt and a protest of man against the progressive bareness of the walls in the rooms of life—a deep hatred of science, which strips humanity of all personal and individual significance, reducing the human species to a few chemicals, a collection of atoms whirling in empty space. Man just cannot tolerate this deep depersonalization that has been going on, not only in science but also in technology. Everything in the laboratory and in the factory seems to point to man's meaninglessness and nothingness. No wonder, then, that as a counterreaction to this degradation of human status there came the rebels in thought, men like Kant who stubbornly installed the human mind as the generator and creator of all reality. When man really was in a state of organic harmony with the universe, as in the Hebrew Bible and in much of Greek philosophy, and even in the Middle Ages, no such exaggerated approach to the human intellect as making it the total guarantor of reality was needed.

How extreme much of modern thought about man is! For example, in Kierkegaard you have an outlook which bypasses society and man's duties toward it. All that is real is yourself in relation to God. Well, that is a very comfortable doctrine if you want to escape involvement with other human beings, with all the sexual and aggressive possibilities of that involvement. It is far better to despair with God—far better. This approach to the universe, which emphasizes solitude and embraces solitude as though there were no escape, is in a sense a return to the domicile of infancy—to that blessed omnipotence of the child ego that has been so well described by psychoanalysts like Otto Fenichel. If you alone exist, or you and God alone exist, then you don't have any burdens of complicated responsibility and moral action toward brothers and friends and neighbors. This subjectivism, which is a denial of human relatedness of man to man, is a trick, an essential untruth.

Subjectivism, of course, is only one of the poles of reaction to the threat of our times. There is another counterreaction formation in the intellectual realm. That is the antiseptic objectivity of many modern scientists. It is against this abdication of the individual personality that Kierkegaard and his followers have really rebelled. The mathematician juggling his symbols, the physicist dealing with his formulas is safe from all entangling emotional alliances, personal and psychological. He has become in his laboratory a Svengali hypnotizing nature and enjoying that domination. It is so satisfying to the power drive in man, and nature offers such a hard and satisfying target for all our aggressions. The scientist can pummel nature and dissect nature and blast nature at will. That is not the case with one's emotions. It certainly is not the case with the emotions of one's fellows. You cannot banish them so easily. Therefore, if you are a scientist, you deny and ridicule emotion and you turn to the very safe realm of your laboratory and to your experiments with indifferent atoms.

All this subjectivism and alienation and existentialism are grandiose lies, for we human beings inevitably live not isolated but in contexts. We often do not and should not like the contexts in which we find ourselves, but we cannot conjure them away. We moderns have tried to be such magicians and medicine men with all our homeopathic magic—reading out of existence whatever destroys our serenity, be it matter or mind, society or God. The truth of life is found in the principle of contextualism or relatedness. Now, many forms of relatedness are very poignantly defeating. That is why the writers of the world who celebrate and commemorate man's aloneness like to deny this law of life, just as the Christian Scientists try to deny matter and evil. But we are as much the product of relatedness as the cell is the product of molecules and the atom is a prisoner of its patterned electrons. We all of us live in a "field world" humanly as well as physically and chemically.

CHAPTER FOUR

Morality and Immorality

THE HOPE FOR A BROADER BASE

We certainly live in an age of enormous moral confusion. How many of us have almost completely lost the sense of right and wrong, dismissing questions of good and evil as matters of mere personal taste? How many say that all ethical judgments are purely relative and that we can be excused for almost every action as a decree of heredity or environment? Now, these are very comforting exits from personal moral responsibility. I suspect their validity. I maintain the inner necessity of the moral adventure for man, convinced as I am that human nature can discover neither peace nor happiness without allegiance to basic moral standards.

Not that I blame our generation for its perplexity about what is moral and what is immoral. We have all of us been exposed to such contradictory advice and such chaotic experiences. We have regarded it as "smart" to rebel against mid-Victorian standards of decency and integrity. The words "sin" and "righteousness" have practically been dropped from the vocabulary not only of thought but of action. The moral coins of virtue and of vice have been traded in at the counter of psychological novelty, and for those eternal and time-tested treasures we have

101

taken in exchange the shiny and glittering counterfeit coins called "emancipation," "sophistication," "moral liberation."

Yet do we not today feel like ethical beggars with this counterfeit money of modernity jingling in our pockets, unable to buy us any peace, harmony, abiding joy? What, then, shall we do?

We can try to look at the moral story and find out where we have gone wrong and how we can find our way again to the true treasure-houses laden with the coinage of goodness.

The changing history of morality in the Western world is a fascinating one indeed. There have been many "mood swings" in humanity's feelings about right and wrong. In the Bible man's conscience was identified with the "still small voice of God." Our Old Testament ancestors developed a healthy-minded sense of sin which they identified with a separation from God, a rebellion against His moral will for man's fulfillment and society's growing harmony. Later the Western world under the influence of the Greeks and the Romans, themselves filled with justifiable guilt at tyranny and barbarism and profoundly affected by the teachings of Augustine and his Christian followers, came under the spell of a growing anxiety. The anguished conscience of Western culture was climaxed during the Protestant Reformation by the teachings of Luther and Calvin about man's depravity and worthlessness. Interestingly enough, however, sin became quite parochial in Luther and in Calvin. Whereas the Hebrew Bible had made quite clear that not only adultery but economic injustice, the misuse of power, the indifference to the needy, and the idolatry of one's self as a little god constituted unrighteousness, the spokesmen of religion at the time of the Reformation terribly circumscribed the nature of sin. For the last several centuries, in fact, religious teachers have largely equated sin with sensuality, as though the evils of the flesh were Satan's major changes of garment. In our industrial and capitalistic society, the often ugly, non-sensual passions of men in their quest for power have been garbed in the waistcoats of eminent respectability. Avarice has been bemedaled as Industry; Economic Aggression has been decorated and knighted as Thrift; Pride has been silk-hatted as Individual Initiative. Immorality has been identified with Sexuality quite often to the exclusion of the vast abuses of power and display of human cruelty in the economic and social world complacently left by both religion and philosophy under the dominion of moral outlaws and jungle rulers whether disguised as "robber barons" or "political tyrants."

Actually Western culture for the last several centuries has not been too tormented by moral anguish. Sin was put in its proper corner, and man, dazzled by the dream of conquering the world and mastering newly discovered continents, became preoccupied with material things and lost any consuming interest in Heaven or Hell. Modern man to a large degree has been a disciple of Francis Bacon, swaggering along the highways of adventure and power with wealth in one hand and science in the other. Not long after the Reformation with all of its puritanical motifs man became so preoccupied with colonization and industrialization that he had little energy left for deep soul-searching or moral reflection. Up until the First World War Western civilization was pretty much like a cocksure adolescent intolerant of the parental tutelage of past ages and growingly confident that its muscles and its mind would prove almost omnipotent against the obstacles of nature. This was another mood swing in the zigzag story of morality in the Western world. Religion was assigned a very minor role in the drama of modernity. Conscience as the "still small voice of God" was banished to the wings of the theater of Being. Man did not take too seriously the gloomy diagnosis of Protestantism, of human nature as hopelessly sinful. He who sailed the seas and conquered colonies and built factories certainly did not feel himself impotent or hopeless. More and more he became inflated with a sense of self-importance. During the eighteenth and nineteenth centuries a very blithe confidence appeared in Western philosophy: that man's domineering Reason would solve all moral problems. Science testified that the growing might of the wheel and the factory, the test tube and the retort, would chemically dissolve all the spiritual and ethical doubts of men. Life began to be lived in the fond hope that inner anguish would be washed away by the cool waters of education, science, and technology.

In retrospect, that touching faith that a little more education, a little more science, and a little more rationalism would dissolve all moral perplexities does seem rather absurd. How naïvely optimistic were our grandfathers in their conviction that humanity could enter a Rousseauean paradise free of the burdens and ethical clothes with which civilization weighs us down, free to gambol as moral nudists in a kind of Garden of Eden innocence.

The two World Wars through which we have lived are responsible for another mood swing—from optimism to pessimism. Our age has seen so many illusions shattered. Man is not the easily domesticated animal that the gentle advocates of Enlightenment believed him to be. Liberalism has been increasingly terrorized by the grinning skulls of primitivism and barbarism that even the most emancipated contemporary carries within him consciously or unconsciously as relics of his evolutionary past. Today, as a kind of reaction to the poignant optimism of the last century, man has burdened himself with the hunchback of new and darker illusions. Poets and theologians delight in beating their sinful breasts while singing the sad song of man's total depravity. The pendulum has swung from a consuming confidence in human nature and its power to a destructive deprecation of man wallowing in impotence. Everywhere one turns today in the realm of literature one encounters Satan either in good standing as the fallen angel of God or garbed in the atheistic sport costumes of the existentialists. Guilt hangs heavy over the human scene. The rhyme and the meter of poetry are weighted with the accents of doom and evil.

It is not too farfetched to say that man has been a manic-depressive as far as morality is concerned. Sometimes he has been in the trough of despondency about his sinfulness and evil, and then his mood has shifted, tossing him high upon the wind of self-confidence to the summit of pride and power. These mood swings about morality will never be cured until we understand more clearly the nature of human ethics—not only its origin but its infinite potentialities. Today the confusion about what is good and evil is like an impassable mountain on man's journey. Some thinkers seriously maintain that the moral sense of man is merely the residue or sediment of social mores. Some philosophers reduce moral distinctions to private taste and personal preference, purely subjective in nature. They take away all the grandeur of goodness, and label it a prejudice of social convention, the illegitimate child of a casual romance between heredity and environment. They say that man's moral feelings are no more permanent or objective than his accidental liking for a certain kind of music or his acquired taste for olives. We have to wrestle with this moral nihilism. Is it true that man's ethical yearnings are incidental and accidental to his nature?

Few seem to know what to believe about man himself, whether he is merely a higher animal or a fallen angel, a complex chemical compound, a plaything of heredity, a moral zero, or a helpless cork tossed on the waves of differing oceans, sometimes tranquil, sometimes tempestuous.

As for myself, I believe that man is not a helpless cork, a mere chemical compound, a slave to environment or heredity, but that he is a creature of God, endowed by his Creator not merely with inalienable rights but with inalienable *qualities* as well. Man is a morality-seeking creature even as he is a truth-seeking creature. God has fashioned the world full of many things, rocks that are hard, mountains that are towering, seas that are shimmering, and man who is haunted restlessly until he achieves a rich measure of beauty, of truth, and of goodness. The conscience within man is as much a part of him as the intellect within him. At birth, these are both merely potential, but in the very protoplasm of the human species there is the hunger and the need for moral fulfillment and intellectual growth as well as for biological nutriment. It is absurd to limit man to the realm of truth and to blind our eyes to his equal appetite for goodness. Even as the plants turn to the light of the sun for their chlorophyll, so do men turn to the light of the sun of goodness for moral chlorophyll with which to sustain themselves. It is of course true that many human beings in their folly never develop their potential intellects, remaining serfs to ignorance. Likewise, many never develop their potential consciences, remaining slaves to passion or cruelty. This does not negate, however, the reality of the "still small voice of God" present within the very germ plasm of humanity any more than the small tender flame of intelligence which flickers at birth in every normal infant can be denied.

106

Now, what happens to this potential conscience? How does it grow? Wherein is it stunted or twisted? The eminent biologist Julian Huxley, in his book entitled *A Touchstone for Ethics,* wrestles with this problem of the origin and early history of the moral sense in us. He traces it back to the relationship that the infant has with the first representative of the social world—its mother. The baby loves the mother deeply but likewise resents her in moments of deprivation and frustration. Out of this earliest contact of the human infant with the mother figure, out of this creative conflict between love and hate, there emerge the feelings of right and wrong, the first elements of the childish conscience. Conflict is necessary, then, in order for a sense of right and wrong to become incorporated into our very substance. Paradoxically enough, it is quite fortunate that man should in infancy have the capacity for feeling guilt born initially out of the sense of disappointing a beloved mother and rooted of course always in the God-given capacity for making ethical distinctions. No guilt, no goodness. This formula is proved in the case histories of moral delinquents who have had no true mother figure with whom to relate themselves and thus grow up without any sharp sense of right and wrong.

Blessed, then, is the human being who has had a wonderful mother and father wise enough to train and develop a childish conscience, the forerunner of our adult moral code. The great gift that God has given us, if we would but realize it, is this ability to take our childish conscience—which has been molded and shaped on the anvil of a mother's commandments and prohibitions, a father's wishes and orders—and ourselves beat out new shapes of goodness upon the anvil of our own growing reason with the creative hammers of our own enlarging experience. The truth that we all have to learn is never to rest content with the childish conscience more or less given to us by our parents or the adult world, but to keep the flame of sensitivity at white heat in the smithy of our own intellect and to remove some of the metal that is dead weight and add new moral metal with every decade of our growth.

The great mistake of contemporary life is that we have made such a virtue of intellectual growth while almost totally ignoring the necessity of conscience growth. We have failed to understand that individual evolution can take place not only in mental but in moral power. The earth tragically today is full of people who remain fixated on a childish level of conscience. What an illusion has blinded the human race: that our conscience is given to us once and for all at birth and we ourselves have to do little or nothing about it. Quite fallaciously we think of our conscience as though it were similar to our eyes, our ears, our sense of sight and smell. The truth is that our moral capacity is purely potential and needs strenuous training, education, development. It is certainly not an organic power that comes to us at birth, like breathing, which demands little attention from us as long as we live.

A revolution has to take place in our thinking about morality. We have to become as sensitive about being moral morons as we are now anxious about being intellectual idiots. We do not trust nature to give us the fruits of reason without effort on our own part. We are sent to school to spend long years in preparation for a vocation, a profession, an art. That same wisdom must now be applied to the education of the moral sense within us. All that we get from our parents is the first edition of a conscience. We ourselves have to create our revised editions as we grow, deleting the errata of infancy and adolescence. We have to learn how to change, discipline, and mature our ideas of goodness within us even as we strive to mature our ideas of nature and matter as we grow older. Very few people are satisfied with the understanding of science that they possess when they are twelve years old. They try to go on and master newer theories of chemistry and physics. If they find this difficult or impossible they at least remain silent in the presence of greater authority. Knowing their own incompetence, they defer to the experts in the field, respecting the laboratory masters. Most intelligent people, however, try to keep up with newer developments in science and medicine, dissatisfied with their childish fantasies about physical nature. It has become the fashion in America for us to want to develop intellectually. We are ashamed of our ignorance. That shame is a very creative source of growth. But ought we not to be more ashamed of an unripe, immature conscience than of an unripe, immature mind? As far as the intellect is concerned, we can specialize and hand over responsibility to experts who will create new medicines for us or invent new machines and labor-saving devices in our behalf. In an age where there is much division of labor we can delegate many intellectual tasks to others but we certainly cannot delegate moral tasks to others. Vicarious intelligence is possible; vicarious conscience is not. Every one of us, as long as he lives, affects himself and his life circle by what his conscience inspires him to do or not to do. We can afford neither intellectual nor moral indolence.

This is the revolution that is needed in our age—the understanding that we ought to be far more unhappy about remaining on the kindergarten level of conscience than about remaining on the childish level of information and intellect. Yet few realize this truth. We are poignantly proud of our degrees and diplomas and equally proud of our growth in the mastery of matter and nature. But have we seen that the potential conscience in us requires just as much attention as the potential intellect—probably more if the world is to be saved? We can hire a mathematician to solve a difficult equation for us; we can engage a chemist to fashion a new organic compound for our needs. We cannot really buy anyone to make our moral choices for us. A world that is intellectually mature but morally infantile is on the road to ruin.

The true hope is that we will now for the first time perceive that there is in us not only mental power but moral power waiting to be trained and educated in accordance with our growing experience and in the light of our widening horizons of reason.

Since according to my theory conscience is not something given ready-made to man, but is something achieved by man as he grows and matures, it should be obvious that there can be little, stunted and pygmy consciences in men and women as well as ever-evolving moral luminaries within us. When man morally grows from childishness to maturity he evolves from a warm love of one human being—his mother—to a tender life-affirming regard for many human beings. He throws off many childish burdens of unrealistic guilt and is educated to understand the necessity of loving himself wisely and of forgiving others. Man becomes maturely moral when he loves his neighbors with their shortcomings even as he loves himself with his shortcomings.

How, then, does a mature conscience reveal itself? What do I mean by morality and immorality? I would like to define morality as the concern of a person for the achievement of a worthwhile life for himself and his immediate circle of loved ones, extending out into a commitment to the larger human circle without exclusion of race, creed, or color. In the second place, morality is the willingness to struggle for that which ought to be, the ability to pursue an ideal that shall outlast one's own day on earth.

Immorality is the opposite of these two aspirations. It shows itself in a self-centered concern for one's own power and pleasure with an indifference to the fulfillment and happiness of others; and in a dull acquiescence in that "which is," the status quo with all its evils, rather than a passionate battle for that which "ought to be" with all of its potential moral goods.

Now, immorality is not sexual irregularity only. Such a definition is merely a clever device by which modern men and women legitimatize many of their worst antisocial trends. If you can confine evil to the sexual realm and allow your pride and aggressions and cruelties to run rampant, you have made quite a good bargain. You can get the reputation of being a "good person" by following the conventional code of respectability while pursuing many subtle demonic pathways.

I would say rather that a person is truly immoral when he wastes his own potentialities and the resources of other people, when he abuses himself psychologically and spiritually and misuses the men, women and children in the circle of his influence. The philosopher Kant maintained that we should treat other people as ends in themselves, not as means to our own personal goals. This for him was one of the great laws of morality. It contains a truth but one that has to be qualified and modified. Now, man is constitutionally a user of material. He metabolizes his food and he consumes the air. So, ofttimes, he metabolizes himself and tries to consume others. How evil it really is to spend our lives eating ourselves or tearing others. Of course, a certain amount of subtlety is required to discern the situations in which we legitimately should use others as means to our ends. A sick person should use a surgeon as the means to renewed health. A person in hunger for the beauty of art should use the great artists of the past and present as the means to aesthetic inspiration.

What is immoral, however, is when we *habitually* use our loved ones as pawns on the chessboard of our passions, hungers, and ambitions, instead of regarding them as creative partners in love and work.

This is a great tool age and a great commodity age. No wonder that we often deal with our children as though they were tools for our prestige and power—no wonder that we buy and sell friends, family, co-workers as marketable commodities in our search for psychological profit. The ethical danger of a commercial society is that we shall come to deal with ourselves and with our neighbors as things and as commodities instead of as persons, when in the words of Martin Buber, we shall have an "I-It" instead of an "I-Thou" relationship to people.

Make no mistake about it. We who live in such a commercial age do treat human lives often as bales of cotton in a glutted market wasting away on the scales of bankruptcy. A deeper psychological explanation for our treating other people as commodities is that we form the habit in childhood of using our parents and the whole adult world as the means to our imperious ends. Sometimes we never outgrow those infantile habits of looking at the world in terms of what it can give us, of how much "milk" in the form of success or approval we can force from the breast of society. As children also we often were afraid of being used as the instruments of our parents' ambitions or desires. Perhaps in adult life we attack first and attempt to use other people as means to our ends in order to escape being attacked or used by them. Maturity in the moral realm will come when we attain the ability to regard fellow human beings and ourselves not as commodities but as creative co-workers.

A new era will be born when we become wise enough, furthermore, to see that immorality is not only improper sexual indulgence but the improper wastage of human resources, our own or those of other people.

When are we immoral toward ourselves? When we needlessly warp ourselves through self-hatred and obsessive guilt feelings about the imperfections that are inherent in life, when we cripple our potentialities for growth by the crushing blows that we inflict on our minds and hearts through needless feelings of inadequacy, inferiority, anxiety.

When are we immoral to others? When we try to dominate, to possess, and to tyrannize over our wives, children, employees, friends, or when we try to diminish other people either by our words or deeds. You are acquainted with the grotesque headhunters among the primitive tribes still alive in parts of the world who shrink human heads almost to pinpoint size. Well, there are spiritual headhunters among civilized nations who by words and actions try to shrink their neighbors and their loved ones to pinpoint insignificance. The attempt to make our neighbors pygmies through the destructive chemicals of our gossiping tongues or our acid-like criticism is certainly a widespread moral evil in our insecure society. The even worse exploitations and injustices which darken the social and economic realms are the moral flaws of individuals magnified a thousandfold on the social screen. The truth is that while immorality begins at home it never ends there. People who have never learned how to educate their childhood consciences continually search for scapegoats for their inner frustrations—a wife, a child, a group like the Negroes or Jews, or whole nations. The evils of an immoral conscience spill over into acids that burn not merely the faces of those nearest to us but, as in our own time, the very face of the earth in war and tyranny. The smoke of concentration camps and cremation factories, the cruelties of the police state abroad, as well

113

as the hunger of the slums and the poverty of sharecropping families here at home, are all the tragic progeny, the brutal brood, of man's stunted and twisted moral sense. Yet, strange as it seems, man is a creature haunted by the moral dream.

Actually, man's detours into immorality, his perversions of justice, are quite different from the simple and uncomplicated savagery of the animal. Man is the only creature on earth that lives in the future as well as in the present, in the world of imagination as well as in the arena of action. Our species is unique in its capacity for being haunted by an ideal. We can flee from that ideal or pervert it, but even our perversion of it is a subtle and unintended tribute to its power over us. There is something within us that will not allow us to remain content with evil or cruelty. There is something in our inner character that sweeps us along many broken highways toward horizons of genuine goodness. God has made man a haunted creature, haunted as long as he wastes his own powers and destroys the gifts of other people. Life does not permit him forever to dwell comfortably among the weeds of triviality or to rock on the tumbled-down porch of Being, facing the fruitless orchard of self-centeredness and moral defeat.

True morality is the drive for self-fulfillment, the concern for the fulfillment of others, and the quest for ideals beyond our present attainment. We become good when we treat ourselves with legitimate self-respect, discipline our angers and lusts, and liberate ourselves from the false demands of perfection and of guilt; and when we treat others with equally profound respect, aiding them to attain love, knowledge, and inner satisfaction. Morality says, "Look upon other people not as the subway to your private way-stop, as the train to your terminal of desire; use other people not as boats carrying you to your selfish shore on the other side of the river of life; see your loved ones and your neighbors as the end of your journey, the destination of your human travels, the place where you can get off and rest and fulfill yourself; act toward other people as though they were the home for you and themselves alike."

We ought to become skillful enough to understand that if other human beings eke out their lives in frustration, hate, and poverty, we ourselves shall be warped and twisted, for we do belong to one another and are involved in each other's pain and destiny. The carbon monoxide of unhappiness always seeps into our own consciousness, making us uneasy even while it kills others.

To summarize my thinking up to this point, I would say that we must become as brilliant in maturing our consciences as in deepening our intellects. It is taken for granted that we must revise our conceptions of nature and matter as we grow in knowledge, but man has not yet learned that he should revise his notions of good and evil as he grows in wisdom. Too many men and women walk the streets of the earth with infants' consciences bound to highly trained intellects. A new day will dawn for our Earth when we become as sensitive and as ashamed of a childish conscience as of a childish cosmology. Certainly mankind that has learned through discipline how to split the atom should not find it impossible to master cruelty and achieve creative compassion for one's own potentialities and for the need of fulfillment that lives and burns in every human heart.

There is no reason for pessimism about our moral adventure. Man is not a static creature imprisoned forever within an unchanging room. Actually the great words in contemporary thought are "process" not "substance," "dynamism" not "fixity." The experimentalism of science shows us that life moves, man evolves, the universe progresses. The fact that the scientists of our day are speaking about probability and indeterminacy is a blessing rather than a curse. A planet in which everything would be fixed and certain would offer no real room for growth or change. Fortunately our planet is a plastic ball, giving birth to many new shapes with the time flow of the ages.

Evolution, we are told, stopped thirty million years ago with the insects and the mammals, but with the coming of man the world took on a new lease on life. Progress is not illusion. Man's intellect is the lamp and light that makes up for all the darkness of the planet. It is human intelligence which penetrates the process of the world, makes it grow, encourages it to achieve new qualities of luminous meaning. There is no need for despair. Man is not doomed to fixity, finality, hopelessness. Biology verified in its laboratory what Judaism intuitively sensed thousands of years ago: that the future is open, not closed, and that with the birth of the human species a dynamic restlessness, a creative ferment entered the bloodstream of the stars.

We are learning many wonderful lessons today, even in this dark age. Biologists like Sinnott of Yale and Huxley of England have proved that the democratic dream is rooted in our genes, that the idea that difference is valuable is validated by the discoveries of the sciences of men. Our temperaments and our physiques are irreducibly plural; the world is blessedly made up of a number of things, each uniquely valuable.

True, man is a creature of conflict; his bipolarity is a blessing in disguise. If he felt no inner struggle between love and hate, he would never achieve a sensitivity to guilt or an awareness of goodness. Without the lifelong tension between the north and south poles of morality and immorality, men would be no whit different from the lifeless stone, the withered plant.

Not only biologists but psychiatrists will provide us with a new sophistication. In our century, men and women need no longer remain tragically innocent about their drives and impulses. They will perceive as never before that the drive for achievement can be transformed into the idol of power, that the drive for love can be metamorphosed into a shabby and often degrading sensuality. Suspicion of our motives can become the beginning of goodness. Parents will learn to become suspicious of their power drives and of the masquerades of love by which they hide themselves from their offspring. In this age of psychological sophistication, fathers and mothers will learn the primary lesson: not to overload the growing generation with the heavy bags of guilt or to shackle them with the iron chains of needless repression.

Men and women today can definitely be cured of cruelty and self-hatred. That is one source of hope for a new morality. I am convinced that if we can but outlive the atomic bomb, we will be able to achieve consciences approaching the adult, and societies made up of adult men and women will heal many present psychic wounds and diseases.

There literally is no limit to the horizons of goodness that men can yet achieve. It is not only the social sciences but the physical sciences that will eliminate the selfishness, for example, born in past ages of scarcity. Men and women were compelled by famine and hunger to hoard things and to exploit one another when there was not sufficient knowledge of the earth, of irrigation, of water power, and atomic energy.

Today a new environmental revolution is under way. In this technological age, which can provide heat for all, food for all, security for all, most of the hatred and selfishness born in the long epochs of human scarcity will wither away. Just as no one today fights in America for access to typhoid-free water because good water is as free as the air we breathe, so in the decades to come people everywhere will cease fighting for the good things of the earth that the magicians of physics and chemistry will yet make possible in this age of abundance.

We have learned how to plan cooperatively in the world of physical science. We have learned how to plan for victory in war. We can yet learn how to plan for the birth of a morality that will bring fulfillment to ourselves and our neighbors, in which we shall live together as men always should have lived, with hate sublimated into love and with disease and injustice as the only enemies and targets of our energy.

The time will yet come when the whole human family shall inhabit a new Heaven and a new Earth, inspired and sustained by the Power who makes for salvation, by God who implants within us the hunger and the appetite for life fulfilled, for morality attained, a hunger that shall yet be satisfied as life shines more and more into the perfect day.

CHAPTER FIVE

The Road to Inner Serenity

LOVE IS RELATEDNESS

"So teach us to number our days, that we may apply our hearts unto wisdom." Indeed, if we are ever to find inner serenity, we must discover a new heart of wisdom both in our personal adjustment and in our social attitudes.

One thing that we all need today is a profounder understanding of what we human beings really are and what we most deeply need. What are we? We strange human beings, mixture of clay and clouds, are the supreme wanters of the universe. We want many things: food, shelter, physical security, and work for our hands and our minds. But two of the deepest needs of man we ofttimes do not clearly comprehend and may not even be aware that we need: true love and true tolerance.

The first fundamental truth about our individual lives is the indispensability of love to every human being. By "love" I mean relatedness to some treasured person or group, the feeling of belonging to a larger whole and of being of value to the life of other men. The source of all the basic anxieties in human nature is a feeling of being alone and helpless in a hostile world, and the first compulsion of life is the weaving of a stable pattern of relationship between ourselves and our parents and all of those who in time take the place of our parents—the beloved, the friend, the co-worker. Science, as a matter of fact, teaches us today that we can understand the universe only in terms of relatedness, that things are nothing in themselves, in isolation, that even the atom has significance only in some pattern of organization. Carbon atoms, for example, form charcoal when related in one way and become diamonds when related in another. Everywhere we turn in the laboratory, whether in physics or chemistry or biology or even in psychology, we find that isolation is impossible and that relationship is everything. A lone atom is a meaningless atom. A related atom is the building stone of nature. A lone human being is a destroyer of values; a related human being is the builder of the Divine Kingdom.

What the law of gravity is to stars and sun, the law of love is to men and women. What attraction and repulsion are in space, approval and rejection are in human society. We cannot live well, happily, adjustedly without the feeling of our importance to the present or to the future. Even the martyr in the concentration camp, the saint in prison, the lonely heretic divorced from the approval of his age, relate themselves in imagination to wiser men and women who will come after and who will build upon their sacrificial offerings. We all of us retain our sanity by the conviction that we are needed today and tomorrow, and by the memory of love that we have experienced—given or received—which already has become blood of our blood and spirit of our spirit.

Do you want proof of the indispensability of affection, approval, interrelationship to the good life? Then look at this world of hatred, aggression and war. It has been made by loveless men who have taken vengeance upon a world which has rejected them and which they reject. Do you want to know what happens to the soul that never knows the warmth of simple affection, shared laughter, mutual approval, but only isolation, resentment, destruction? Then turn to the peerless navigator of the soul of man, Shakespeare. In *King Richard III* and in *King Henry VI,* he portrays the character of a certain man, physically deformed, who found an outlet for his energy in hate, since no one gave it to him in love. The villain was born then as he is now, out of frustrating aloneness:

> *I have no brother, I am like no brother;*
> *And this word "love," which greybeards call divine,*
> *Be resident in men like one another,*
> *And not in me: I am myself alone.*

"I am myself alone." The villain feels himself cut off from the rest of mankind and deep within his heart knows that his loneliness is the source of his pain, his hatred, his vengeance. Richard tries to console himself and to reassure himself that he is self-sufficient, needing no one to share his life and heart; but his reassuring words sound empty to his ears:

> *What do I fear? myself? there's none else by:*
> *Richard loves Richard; that is, I am I. . . .*
> *I shall despair. There is no creature loves me;*
> *And if I die, no soul will pity me.*

Shakespeare, with his incomparable insight into the human soul, realized that there can be no good life without relatedness; that the man who is forced to live in isolation from his fellow beings will, in the words of Richard, "come to bite the world," determined to prove a villain, to bring pain and war and bloodshed as the personal assertions of his power; the tragic coin with which to pay back a loveless destiny.

As we turn the pages of literature we find this first need of the individual—the need of relatedness to some other human beings —expressed again and again. We find it in Rolland's Jean-Christophe, as he is discovering the compensation for life's injustices in his relationship to Otto: "His heart was singing: 'I have a friend! I have a friend!' " We find it in Thomas Wolfe's work: "Where shall the weary rest; where shall the lonely of heart come home? Where shall we cease being lost; lost and naked? When we are loved and wanted."

The primary tragedy of life is rejection. The primary joy of life is acceptance, approval, the sense of appreciation and companionship of our universal comrades. Many men do not understand that this need for fellowship is really as deep as the need for food, and so they go throughout life accepting substitutes for genuine, warm, simple relatedness. The Don Juans, eternally seeking some new object of love, the men and women desperately trying to lose themselves in drink, promiscuity, sensuality —in all of the excesses of flesh and power—are, more often than we suspect, lonely children, lost and naked, in a world that has never woven any bonds for them and that has relentlessly driven them down the empty corridors of the years, desolate and alone.

When we are accepted, approved, needed, by those who know all about us and like us anyway, we have the first inkling of the peace that transcends understanding.

Everywhere we turn, we see this law of relatedness as the first law of life. We saw it among the bombed children of Europe, who could stand almost anything but desertion and rejection.

We saw it among the young soldiers and sailors who went into the jaws of death, sustained only by the inarticulate but infinitely precious sense of brotherhood and shared purpose and mutual value. We see it in the hungry eyes of men and women in all walks of life, seeking the bread and the water of our approval, our encouragement, our assurance that they are needed and that we treasure them.

National isolation has proved to be the father of tyranny. Emotional isolation of man from man is the father of tragedy; it requires no hidden wisdom to learn this first rule of the good life. Almost all human beings have hidden within them a fountain of affection, a spring of generous impulses. The universe has made us potentially altruistic, capable of real interest in other human lives. Do we want inner adjustment and serenity? Let us open the portals of our own hearts and really learn that as we give, we shall receive more in return. As we share, we shall together, in all of the common ways of our life—in laughter, in work, in friendship, in marriage—find the mutual encouragement, the assuaging of the wounds that life inflicts on all of us and thus "apply our hearts unto wisdom."

The first need of the individual in his personal adjustment is relatedness in love to other human beings. It is true that in order to gain love we have to make many renunciations, just as the child has to surrender many of its wild drives in order to gain approval and affection. All human beings have to learn how to adapt themselves to the wishes of others, to accept the social norms of their day. Many times, however, we are made miserable because too much renunciation is demanded of us.

The second great need of individual life is the tolerance of each other's differentness. The world is full of intolerance—not only of the opinions of others but of what is worse: the essence and the uniqueness of others. The father who forces his artistic son into his business, the mother who rivets the daughter to her service by the steel chains of pity and of guilt, subtly refusing to permit the daughter a life of her own—are these not well-known examples of a private imperialism? Many there are who cannot conquer any foreign territory, but who make those nearest and dearest to them pay tribute all of their lives to their dominating whims, their personal caprices. What is not so well known is that this disease of intolerance spreads throughout an entire society, and not only in the parent-child relationship. Many a fine and cultured husband or wife has placed his partner in the straitjacket of his dominating desires, and in the name of love demands unconditional surrender.

If we are ever to have a serene and adjusted individual life, we must rebel against totalitarianism and imperialism, whether in the political or in the personal realm of experience. We should rebel on the grounds of religion and of what it teaches us. We should proclaim these fundamental truths to those who even unconsciously want to make us slaves to their patterns: God has made each man and woman an individual sacred personality, endowed with a specific temperament, clothed with the flesh and blood of differing needs, hungers, dreams. This is a variegated, pluralistic world, where no two stars are the same and every snowflake has its own distinctive pattern. God, apparently, did not want a regimented world of sameness. That is why creation is so manifold.

So is it with us human beings. Some are born dynamic and restless; others placid and contemplative. One man's body is that of a wrestler—thick-muscled, strong, vibrant, needing far greater physical outlet than does the pale poet or the gaunt ascetic. One man's temperament is full-throated with laughter; another's vibrates to the sad chimes of gentle melancholy. Our physiques are different, and that simple difference ofttimes drives us into opposing fulfillments of our natures, to action or to thought, to passion or to denial, to conquest or to submission. There is here no fatalism of endowment. We can change and prune and shape the hedges of our personalities, but we dare not fail to rebel against the sharp shears being wielded by other hands, cutting off the living branches of our spirits in order to make our personalities adornments for their dwellings.

Such a program will require a great deal of inner disciplining on our part—this achievement of personal tolerance—for there is a natural egotism by which we justify placing our dear ones in the Procrustean bed of conformity. We tell ourselves that we only want to do good to our dear ones, to soften the sharp edges of their personalities, to make them more attractive, pleasant, amenable. We do not see that we often demand too high a price for our love. We do not realize that injustice does not consist only in gross exploitations and savage inequality. It manifests itself also when one human being tries to swallow up another's personality. It reveals itself in every demand that we make upon others to cease being themselves in order to be made over in our image. Injustice shows itself often in the slow, imperceptible strangling of initiative, of native spirit, of individual differences between husband and wife, parent and child, friend and friend.

The achievement of true tolerance in personal relations is a requisite, not only in ethics, but in the attainment of our own inner serenity. As long as we are unhappy if others do not conform to our wishes and our ideas of what is proper, good, acceptable, we show that we ourselves are not certain of the rightness of our inner patterns. He who is sure of himself is deeply willing to let others be themselves. He who is deeply unstable in his own character must reassure himself by compressing others into his mold.

To recognize that failure at times is the common lot of all men, to see in ourselves and in others the traces of the primitive as well as the promise of the civilized, to admit that our friends' patterns of life, although different from ours, are equally valuable, and because of the very differences indispensable for a rich and varied universe, to recognize that another may be right while we are wrong, is to attain the second great need of individual adjustment—genuine inner tolerance.

We need a heart of wisdom not only in our personal adjustment but also in our social relationships.

Religious Maturity Through God

It is curious and at the same time revealing that men are afraid to indulge too generously in their dreams of a better world. We are burnt children afraid of the fire. We tried before and we failed. That very failure has intensified our guilt feelings about Utopias. Let it not be forgotten, however, that those guilt feelings are the voices of repentance and upon them may be built a far more generous and more decent world order. Many new thoughts are taking root in the minds of men: the conviction that ours is a time of revolution and not only of war, and that flexibility, rather than rigidity, is the demand of the age. The sociologist Karl Mannheim shows that society is always involved in a civil war between those who want to maintain the status quo and those who want to change it. Our age belongs to those who want to change it. That desire for change is itself the product of our collective guilt feeling, our self-accusation at the betrayal of the generous hopes at the end of the last war.

An America that permits exploitation of Negroes in the midst of a war of freedom betrays its sons. An America that permits racial tensions, anti-Semitic prejudices, minority hatreds to grow; an America too busy to concern itself with the health of poor children, the housing of workers, the abolition of slums, is unworthy of the loneliness and the hunger and naked danger of our far-flung battle lines.

May we learn to number our days with such wisdom that under God we shall not grow too weary to create a people's world, with no children hungrily looking on at the feasts of the few, no outcasts separated from our common good, no aggressions undisciplined, no persecutions unoutlawed; to fashion a society with impartial standards of justice, economic and political, above all of the grasping seekers of power, and beyond the reach of any human whim, with the sacred right of change and evolution guaranteed to men and nations—a world that will begin to fulfill the dreams of Isaiah and the promises of Lincoln.

Many men and women who have no difficulty in understanding the need of new individual adjustment and new social vision find it extremely difficult to obtain a heart of wisdom in relation to God. They stumble over that word "God" feeling themselves unable, in any deep sense, to accept Divinity. The reason why Western mankind has found difficulty in believing in the wider horizons of religion is that science, dazzling and arrogant with success, became in the last hundred years like a one-party system of government, usurping all of the authority, prestige and dominion in the state of human thinking. Religion and morality were driven into exile like naked refugees, stripped of significance and status, and the dictator, Science, began to rule the lives of men in truly totalitarian fashion. What it approved received the

127

insignia of reality. What it frowned upon became the object of contempt and the laughingstock in the eyes of the followers of science. Today the tyranny of the intellectual dictatorship is being broken, and the exiles, wandering in outer space, rather shabby and homeless, without the visas and the passports of entry into the country of the modern mind—religion, morality, the realms of the spirit—are being called home, for men are coming to recognize that the land called "reality" can be ruled successfully only by a partnership of science, of art, of religion —not only truth, but beauty and goodness as well.

An interesting example of this chastened and changed mood is revealed in the book by the English philosopher C. E. M. Joad entitled *Good and Evil*. Professor Joad, for thirty years rather like the Clarence Darrow of British thought, a proud agnostic, an assured atheist, reveals himself as a religious penitent, and in a very honest and learned work tells why he joined so many other scientists and intellectuals in a return to the religious quest for God, convinced that man can find peace and self-assurance only as he feels himself buttressed and supported by contact with the Power greater than man.

The question that is in so many minds today is whether we are really justified in believing that there is a wider horizon to which we can become related, that there is purpose and intelligence and perfection in the universe as attributes of a Power greater than man, and that we can rely and depend upon that Power to give us the means of life and of salvation, or, shall we say, that the thought of God is merely a subjective projection of our childish need, the word-spinning of our desperate hunger, the illusion born out of our frightened aloneness. Here we are perhaps in a realm of temperament. Some men, in love with the thought of their own independence and complete self-reliance, will reject every evidence of Divinity because of their own egotistical self-centeredness. Other men and women may too easily make God a reed to lean upon or may make Him in all too human a form, compressing His infinite reality into the mold of childish fancies.

We must not make God the echo of our finiteness. We must not try to photograph Him in the little cameras of our own fragile experience. We must be humble and accept our destiny—that if we are not mystics, gifted in the art of communication with the Ineffable, we shall but continue to stammer and stutter in the presence of the Divine mystery and catch at best only a few glimpses of His Majesty in the order of nature and in the accents of human conscience. Yet we dare to affirm the Power greater than ourselves, even though we cannot exactly define God. Why?

Since we human beings are so limited and our language is always inexact, we know that we can never describe God adequately, but must always use metaphor and analogy in order to interpret Divine Reality. What many people do not understand is that our scientific description of the universe is just as metaphoric as the religious description. Men thought that they were being very exact and scientific when they called the world a great machine. Is that not an analogy? A metaphor? Whenever we speak of reality as a machine or as purely material, we are reading something into the world. Why should we continue to interpret the universe in terms of the lowest that we know rather than in terms of the highest that we experience? Intelligence, purpose and personality, the will to live, the need to love, the yearning to be related—these are just as important clues to reality as atoms and electrons. It sometimes seems to me that our habit of looking at the universe in terms of matter, rather than in terms of purpose and of conscience, is a reflection of our inferiority complex—as though we human beings were not worthy to be regarded as mirrors of the Divine. Perhaps this is a reflection of the spiritual masochism and self-deprecation that has come through the influence of Calvin and Kierkegaard and Niebuhr. There is no logical reason why we should explain reality always by reducing the complex to the simple. Why exalt the atom as the clue to truth and ignore the mind of man?

Why should we not believe that that which is highest in ourselves is a reflection of that which is deepest in the universe— that we are children of a world which makes possible the growing achievement of relatedness, fulfillment, goodness?

Where is there evidence for God in the world? In the fact that there are ideals in existence and conditions that make possible the realization of those ideals. We did not create the world and its value-making potentialities. They were created for us and we are their beneficiaries. The Power greater than man is revealed in a universe where more and more physical laws are uncovered by which mastery and health are achieved. God is revealed also through a world where our spiritual values and ideals are capable of fulfillment when patiently we come to learn their laws—the laws of love, cooperation and relatedness. All of our wishes are not fulfilled—true enough! But the essential ones are capable of fulfillment and our deepest dreams are sustained and undergirded by this majestic universe. "To believe in God is to reckon with life's creative forces and possibilities and to know that there is a Power that supports what is and also drives the world to what ought to be!"

While many men are becoming more humble, more willing to see the wider context of experience, there is no doubt but that at the same time there are real obstacles to acceptance of the new faith in Divinity. While it is true on the one hand that we must turn to a power greater than man as the necessary background of man's values and ideals, nevertheless there is a great temptation to become disappointed and disillusioned with that Power because of the evils of the world. How can we solve this great spiritual problem? By following the skeptics in denying any reality to God? No! Let us look at Judaism, which at its best has always summoned man to become mature in his outlook upon God, even as the child gradually becomes mature in his attitude to his human father.

We do not deny the value and the indispensability of our human parents, even after we have discovered their limitations. We ofttimes feel closer to them in a kind of shared reliance and mutual dependence. The wise Jew throughout the ages did not take the easy road or the obvious road when confronted with the evils of life. He did not say, "Now I know that there is no Divinity." That to him would have been as illogical as to have said after disappointment with his human father that there is no humanity. The wise Jew, in all humility and with the recognition of his finite and limited intelligence, concluded that the evils of the world, particularly the man-made evils, could not have been eliminated by God without His eliminating at the same time the ordered nature of the world, its predictability, and the possibility for man's self-achievement and self-growth. The Jew of the ages never pretended that he had a complete or final answer, either to the good or the evil in existence, but he dared to assert the faith which is as logical as is skepticism, that the sorrows of man are both part of his growing pains and the effects of his supreme blessing, his sensitivity, that which distinguishes him from the lifeless star and from inert stone. If we use analogy, as we must, then we say that just as parents cannot successfully raise a child without hardships and deprivations and the growing bestowal of independent responsibility upon their offspring; just as a human father knows that he must not overprotect his son from the risks and the choices of life, unless that son be a helpless and vacant-eyed moron or idiot, so the greater source of all life, whose offspring we all are, could not make us realize ourselves as men without permitting us all of the risks and dangers which bring both evil and blessings. We need not grow disillusioned with God when we realize that He has placed us in a growing world and eternally provides for us the conditions of our fulfillment and *calls* us, but does not *compel* us, to take advantage of the possibilities of salvation available in His Universe.

In the poetic words of the great Jewish theologian Professor Mordecai Kaplan, who has come to a new understanding of God, not childish and anthropomorphic, but reasoned and mature: "Where is God? He is the Oneness that binds the deeps of space. He is the unity of all that is. He is the creative flame that transforms lifeless substance into thought."

God is in the faith
By which we overcome
The fear of loneliness, of helplessness,
Of failure and of death.

God is in the hope
Which, like a shaft of light,
Cleaves the dark abysms
Of sin, of suffering, and of despair.

God is in the love
Which creates, protects, forgives.

132

His the spirit
Which broods upon the chaos men have wrought,
Disturbing its static wrongs,
And stirring into life the formless beginnings
Of the new and better world.

CHAPTER SIX

Courage: Where It May Be Found

Perspective as a Necessity

Surely one of the absolute necessities of our day is perspective —the art of seeing our individual lives and our social realities in the long-range view. Certainly there is much to justify depression today. We never know from moment to moment what surprises the day will bring. We live in a quicksand era, when our professional and financial and social expectations are often frustrated. The only certain thing is uncertainty. Hardship, the readjustment of our lives, the demands of the unexpected, are the things that we have to live with as individuals now. There do come depressive hours to each one of us, when the barometer of our courage shows very low pressure. It seems to me that when those moments of depression come, we should be prepared with a creative attitude toward them, to know that they are transitory, like an occasional illness in the healthy organism; that perhaps we expect too much of ourselves and do not realize that our emotions are as variable as the weather, and that we should accept these temperamental changes without ascribing permanent importance to them. Furthermore, we should realize that our depressed hours falsify and lie about our true natures. If we are normal, they are not the real self. We are, indeed, each one an omnibus in which many selves jostle each other and our depressed self is usually only an occasional traveler, an infrequent passenger, in the vehicle of our lives.

We must learn to identify not with our despondent, but with our confident moods, not to imagine that the fog of the hour reveals the complete horizon of our destiny. Many times we think that we have lost our courage and are depressed personalities because of tragedies in the outer world. That is only part of the story. There are some men who use social catastrophe as a conventionally acceptable reason for their personal depression, whereas the real source is to be found deep in their own natures. The great Latin poet, Horace, expressed this truth in the words "Unless the vessel is clean, whatever you pour into it turns sour." Many people think that they are worrying about the world, and the truth is that they just have not come to terms with themselves. Harry Emerson Fosdick in his essay "Mastering Depression" quotes a character in a modern novel as follows: "Poor Richard Lovatt worried himself to death, struggling with the problem of himself and calling it Australia."

One way to personal perspective is to "know ourselves," to know that we shall inevitably have dark hours, but that we must discount them in the total reality of our lives: for though we may have depressed hours, we need not become depressed persons.

It is often the knowledge of what other men have faced and how other men have triumphed that gives us the personal perspective and the source of personal courage. Mattathias reminded his sons of what odds Abraham and David had confronted, and how they had triumphed over enemies and loneliness and defeats. We, too, feel the surge of new blood in our veins when we read the biographies of great or of humble men

135

and by identifying with them, learn to be strong or of good courage ourselves. I think of the story of the great musician Handel. A biographer tells us, "His health and his fortunes had reached the lowest ebb. His right side had become paralyzed and his money was all gone. His creditors seized him and threatened him with imprisonment. For a brief time he was tempted to give up the fight—but he rebounded again to compose the greatest of his inspirations, the epic *Messiah.*" I think of the famous painter, Millet. While he was working on his immortal canvas *The Angelus,* he wrote, "We have only enough fuel to last us for two or three days and we do not know how we are going to get any more." Then his mother died, and he could not even raise the carfare to visit her upon her deathbed. He played with the idea of suicide, but sublimated that impulse by drawing a sketch of an artist, lying dead at the foot of his easel, and a woman crying out, "Suicide marks dishonor!" When one sees *The Angelus* today, one does not know how much triumph and long-range courage were mingled with the paints and the brush of the artist.

The self-conquest in the lives of other men becomes infectious and contagious as we read the amazing story of human greatness. The voices of Abraham and of David and of all of their successors call to us in the words of Mattathias of old, "Wherefore, ye my sons, be valiant, and show yourselves men."

There is, it seems to me, a justification for personal courage, in terms not only of the past but also of the future. One of the distinguishing traits of our time has been personal insecurity. There has been among us, particularly in America, an adolescent competitiveness—a feeling that life is a race in which the victory of one must be the defeat of the other. No one can measure how much personal unhappiness and inner cowardice have come from this immaturity of our social outlook, this child-like comparison, this absurd rivalry in every area of life. As our democracy becomes more mature, men have a chance of grow-ing up and of realizing that every person is needed and has some contribution to make.

We need the strength that historical perspective can give us; we need to remember what Emerson said: "The lesson of life is . . . to believe what the years and centuries say, against the hours"—to know that often, at the time of greatest darkness, some unpredictable and surprising heroism or Maccabean de-termination saves the day, and gives a new direction to human-ity. It certainly must have seemed hopeless in Palestine, when the majority of Jews were defeatists and only Mattathias and his little band of followers arose to change the course of history— to save Judaism and Western civilization. You remember that Mattathias could have bought the favor of King Antiochus and could have spared himself and his family bloodshed and hard-ship. Stubbornly those Maccabeans refused to surrender to de-featism and by their valor exploded the myth of the Syrians' invincibility. In every age there have been the Spenglers and Sirokins, prophets of doom, who have been proved wrong by man's resoluteness. In 1806 in Britain, William Pitt the Younger said, "There is scarcely anything around us but ruin and de-spair." In 1848 Lord Shaftesbury said, "Nothing can save the British Empire from shipwreck." In our own country, in 1787, Nathaniel Gorham, delegate from Massachusetts, rose to address the Constitutional Convention and sneeringly asked, "Can it be supposed that this vast country, including the Western territory, will a hundred and fifty years hence remain one nation?" That early American was as pessimistic about this country as the Brit-ish Aristocrats were about Britain in the nineteenth century.

We need not even go so far back in history. In the year 1940, military and political prophets of doom joined in a universal chorus, predicting that Britain could not hold more than three weeks, that Russia would collapse within a few days; that the lights were finally going out in the lamp of civilization. We know now how wrong they were, and our spirits should rise whenever we recall how the destructive forces of tyranny, which threatened to have their own way with degenerate democracy, were brought finally to disaster and defeat. And a great truth about life may be learned from this history: that standing opposed to the destructive, cruel, savage elements in human nature stand other elements that are more powerful, constructive, compassionate, upbuilding facets of our being.

There seems to be a principle of polarity at the heart of the universe, a law of opposites governing the planet. The story of life is not merely that of alternation between summer and winter, sleeping and waking, joy and sorrow, but also good and evil, wrestling through an eternal night. Progress is never direct, simple, one-directional. It takes always the spiral result of advance and retreat—an advance to a higher position. Dualism is the truth about our strange human adventure, and the law of action and reaction applies not only in the realm of matter but in the realm of the spirit as well. The forces of evil thought for a while that they would gain a universal victory over defenseless mankind. The awakening of the constructive, freedom-loving, emancipating phase of human nature should be the answer to all pessimists and all voices of doom. This is an historical perspective that we need for our courage. The great American historian Charles Beard superbly crystallized the hope-giving truth that can console us in our hours of despair. He was asked what major lessons he had learned from history. And he answered, "I have learned four. First, whom the gods would destroy they first make mad with power; second, the mills of God grind slowly, yet they grind exceeding small; third, the bee fertilizes the flower it robs; and fourth, when it is dark enough, you can see the stars."

We are beginning a new historical epoch when men are coming to see that evil is self-defeating; that society cannot be built upon lies; that power without goodness can never succeed; and that tyranny meets its nemesis in the eternal Maccabean quality of human nature—the quality that finds guiding stars of hope when the night is darkest.

One important source of courage in our time is perspective, both personal and social. We have learned how as individuals we must anticipate defeat and depression, as inevitable parts of the human adventure. We can teach ourselves to take the dark hours in our stride and to be confident, both of our own inner resources in surmounting difficulty and in the possibility that in total war as well as in total peace each one of us will have something vital to do, and some achievement to live for. This personal perspective makes us stand upon our feet and face life undauntedly. Furthermore, we have learned some social insight from past history—that every age at moments thought of itself as hopeless and viewed its future with despair, and yet progress did come; we have seen that in our own time, the darkest hours of defeat were merely calling forth the inherent heroism and greatness of democracy; that new lights are kindled in the heavens, when the whole horizon seems to be black with human arrogance and destruction.

I believe that we can find courage not merely in the perspective of the past or the realities of the present but also in our justifiable hopes for the future, and I emphasize the adjective *justifiable,* for I know that new things have taken place under

139

the sun. Primitive culture did at one time in history give way to
literate civilizations. Feudalism did disappear under the impact
of the Industrial Revolution. There have been great and important changes in the way that men live and work and govern
themselves. I cannot blind myself to the truth that the American
Revolution did succeed and did bring a new era of independence
and equality into the Western world. Why, then, should I not believe that further world changes can succeed in spreading independence and equality everywhere?

As a Jew I am persuaded by my whole tradition to believe in
the educability of the human race and in the reality of a better
future; that man can learn from his mistakes and his tragedies,
as indeed man has learned in the past; as he has created new
science, new medicine, new technology, new democratic institu-
tions upon the earth, he can still go on to create better ones.

What then, about courage for the future? What are our realistic assets and resources for the future world? Our greatest asset
is our confidence in ourselves, in our success as the result of
initiative and the human imagination. As a people we have been
taught by experience to believe that nothing is impossible and
that failure is the sign of God's disapproval and of human indolence.

From this America, with its restless drive for achievement, its
Puritan inheritance of moral righteousness, its passion for the
just cause, and its generosity of heart and of granaries, there will
come a fighting faith for mankind and a new victory: a new law
of God.

I see the time coming when new lights shall be lit all over the
world, lit by heroes of freedom everywhere. We have lived
through a time when the modern Antiochus has profaned God's
sanctuary and quenched millions of human candles, profaning

every law of God. We are even now dreaming and working for the day when the universal Menorah shall be lit, and in that candelabrum of hope there shall be the eight candles:

1. The candle of *Human Love* that has transcended hatred.

2. The candle of *Human Security* that has conquered hunger and poverty.

3. The candle of *Human Work* that gives meaning and status to every child of earth.

4. The candle of *Human Liberty* that is free from inner and outer slavery.

5. The candle of *Human Perspective* that has learned how to face fear, meet depression and transcend failure, that walks with the brave and the invincible of all ages.

6. The candle of *Human Fidelity* that gives allegiance to life and that commits its energies to the making of a better world, faithful to man and faithful to God.

7. The candle of *Human Peace* that will indeed use the plowshares and the airplanes to bind together in concord the interdependence of the human family.

8. The candle of *Human Courage* that dares all and endures all; that demands no sudden Utopia but works without surrender for a nobler earth; that kindles an eternal flame that shall never be quenched.

CHAPTER SEVEN

Love in Marriage Today

PERSONAL DESIGNS FOR HAPPINESS

"And they lived happily ever after" is one of the most tragic sentences in literature. It is tragic because it tells a falsehood about life and has led countless generations of people to expect something from human existence which is not possible on this fragile, failing, imperfect earth. The "happy ending" obsession of Western culture is both a romantic illusion and a psychological handicap. It can never be literally true that love and marriage are unblemished perfections, for any worthwhile life has its trials, its disappointments, and its burning heartaches. Yet who can compute the numbers of people who have unconsciously absorbed this "and they lived happily ever after" illusion in their childhood and have thereafter been disappointed when life has not come up to their expectations and who secretly suffer from the jealous conviction that other married people know a kind of bliss that is denied to them?

Life is not paradise. It is pain, hardship, failure and temptation shot through with radiant gleams of light, friendship and love. The rabbis of old understood this truth. We are told in the Talmud that once there was a long debate among the sages as to whether it was better to have been born or not. Certain of the teachers came to the conclusion that it would have been better never to have been born at all, but that, since we are in this life, we must make of it as charming and noble and moral and joyous an adventure as fallible human nature can.

In this mysterious universe man and woman have been placed to unravel the skein of their terrestrial destiny, to spin out the threads of surprises, exaltations, miseries, all intermingled in the silken tapestry of being. Man is not a stone: this is both his fortune and his misfortune. A rock, a piece of inorganic matter, lies inert upon the side of a hill; it feels and desires nothing and therefore escapes all pain; but it also senses neither ecstasy nor conscious awareness. Men and women appear on the horizon coming with the dawn, carrying with them invisible baggage— nerves that can both torment and exalt, muscles than can move and walk and consume space, spirits that can soar heavenward or sink into a purgatory of despair. The most precious part of the baggage which we carry with us is our capacity to love, to feel affection, passion, concern. It is as though God had resolved to compensate us for our taut nerves and our tense anxieties and for all of the dark woods through which we must journey, and had placed within each spirit a beacon light, the capacity to love. As each one of us journeys from east to west, from dawn to sunset, from horizon to horizon, we are made more than clods of earth by our very capacity to suffer and to enjoy. Marriage is a divine institution, giving a more permanent dwelling to love; it is a divine institution because it enables men and women to soften fate's hard blows and to cushion each other against the shocks of despair and loneliness.

If it is true that marriage is a divine institution and a life-long career, it is true too that there are some who do not choose to follow that career. There are men and women who remain unmarried throughout life and who achieve happiness and beauty according to their own unique pattern. Some of the noblest women of the world—Jane Addams or Lillian Wald—were able to live full and creative existences outside the realm of marriage. People may be married and feel themselves the loneliest of the lonely; others who have never experienced wedlock may be among the most joyous, radiant, richly endowed human personalities, and find intense gratification in a multitude of activities—artistic, musical, social.

In contrast, there are multitudes, however, who make tragic failures in the career of marriage. The increase in the divorce rate in this country indicates how necessary it is for us to deal with the problem of love and marriage today and to try to find some pattern for success in this basic social institution. In 1867 there were about 10,000 divorces granted in the United States; in 1937 the number rose to over 250,000. In that same period the population, it is true, increased 300 per cent, but the number of divorces increased 2,000 per cent. A shockingly high proportion of the families of the country are in danger not only of discord but of complete disruption.

Here we are the most literate people in the world, better educated than any of our ancestors, and yet making bitter failures of our personal relationships. This is a mystery until we realize that there is no necessary connection between knowledge and wisdom, between information and insight. Oh, we are a very well-informed people as far as the outer world is concerned, but we have been running away more and more from the wise management of our own inner natures. It is not facetious to say that there are multitudes of people who are better acquainted with the political and internal problems of the day than they are with the more inescapable issues of their own personal relationships.

A man may know *Inside Asia* and *Inside Europe* from cover to cover, but know little of the inside needs, conflicts, dreams of his life partner.

Life does not ask us all to become great statesmen, clever generals, brilliant politicians; it does call upon most of us to become successful husbands and wives. In fact, in this age with its tremendous outer insecurity, its wars, its mass violence, its industrial callousness, love and happiness in marriage are much more necessary to us than ever before. A joyous home becomes a haven of refuge in the storm of disillusionment, frustration, and fear of the future.

What are the obstacles to marital happiness today? What are the things which prevent us from achieving successful marriage? A rabbi inevitably deals with the most intimate problems of human relations and sees many mistakes which he would wish men and women could avoid. How much energy is expended by families in preparation for the wedding, how little thought is given to preparation for the marriage! There is the same tragic impatience in this sphere as in other spheres on the American scene. The ideal in the economic realm has been for so long to get rich quick that we try as well "to get happy quick." The very fact that statistically the largest per cent of marriages are dissolved in their first few years is an indication of this basic truth. To expect marriage to be happy all at once is like expecting a seed to yield its harvest in a day. With the honeymoon we have just matriculated in the school of marriage. We are just at the beginning of the long process of education. How absurd it would be if a child were to demand a complete education within a year! Yet many young people who are beginning a career expect to be graduated with honors after a totally inadequate expenditure of time and of energy. Why should we expect to make a quick adjustment to the marriage group that we have entered when it takes us a lifetime to learn how to adjust ourselves to the other groups in our lives? We spend twenty years in becoming at home in the world. All our childhood and adolescence is devoted to learning the subtle art of adjustment to the demands of society. Marriage is a little microcosm of society. We have no right to expect to learn the art of adjustment to this new world of experience in one year or in ten years.

As a matter of fact, in this new society of marriage, most people have to live through childhood and adolescent phases before they become maritally adult. We have to relive our experiences on every stage of our existence. Now, just as the child has to take time to find his bearings, and to chance the subtleties of the social atmosphere in which he moves and breathes and makes his stumbling acquaintance with reality, and just as the adolescent goes through many moody, rebellious, unhappy stages in making his peace with the world, so should we anticipate in marriage, in this most intimate society, the same difficulties, the same tasks of getting our bearings, making our stumbling acquaintance with the emotional reality of our partner in life through many fleeting moods before we can become one.

No, we do not usually despair or commit suicide when we make our mistakes in our first contacts with the universe of men and of stars. Why should men and women commit marital suicide when they make the inevitable mistakes in their first years of marriage together? The term suicide is not too strong a word. Many individuals do destroy part of themselves and certainly help to destroy the joy, the happiness and the well-being of others when they easily abandon the struggle and lightly forgo the responsibilities of marriage. In this realm, as in every other realm, there must be a strong will to live, a will to survive, to rise above transient pains and frustrations; otherwise there can be no success, no happiness, no true design for living.

Our gossamer romantic dream of marriage does infinitely more harm than good. We somehow are led to expect perfection from life. The fairy tales of childhood people our imagination with Prince Charmings and Sleeping Beauties. We find it difficult later to adjust to life which gives us men and women often lovable, more often fallible. No rabbi can be in the ministry for any length of time without being aware of the illusions with which people come to marriage. All of us have been more or less deluded by false standards. Here is a wife who is continually unhappy because her husband is not a great financial success. Another wife is miserable because her husband is not as versatile, as intellectual, as cultured as another. Here is a husband who is continually comparing his wife with some dream image, some paragon of impossible virtues. Another husband demands that his wife be artist, mother, nurse, mistress, comrade—all to the nth degree of perfection! If one had the power of a dictator for just one hour, one would like to take these men and women and force them to see life as it really is. The pastures which seem greener are really an optical illusion. The basic tragedy of humanity is that while each individual can understand only himself directly, he can know what goes on in other human lives only by inference. We torment ourselves by attributing perfection, joy, happiness to others. They make the same mistake about us. Most human beings do not carry their hearts on their sleeves; all live a life partially of pretense and appearance. Every human being has limits, imperfections, frailities. Happiness is unobtainable until one makes his peace with this emancipating truth.

If I were dictator for an hour, I would compel unhappy wives to realize that while husbands may not be financial tycoons or intellectual giants still they labor hard and work devotedly. For the goal of human life is not only the accumulation of wealth or wisdom; it is the creation of a harmonious, unified, tolerant design with sweetness and mutuality and loyalty as the insignia of achievement. Stop dreaming your dreams of a Prince Charming! He exists only in that never-never land of Peter Pan and Alice in Wonderland.

If I were dictator for an hour, I would let the husband see not only his wife as she is, but all other women as they are, all of them sharing foibles and frailties. I would compel him to realize the preciousness of the devotion, the sacrifice, the love which he has for so long been taking for granted. If I had the power, I would say to many husbands, "How can you expect love and happiness to be yours, when you make so little investment in it, so little expenditure? Marriage also is a career. You could not become a famous lawyer merely by passing the bar examination. You could not become a skilled surgeon merely on receipt of a medical diploma. Why, then, should you expect to become a successful husband merely upon the receipt of a wedding certificate? If you spent as little time on your business or your profession as you spend upon your wife and your family, you would soon be bankrupt. Realize there is nothing automatic about success in marriage; success is not a gift. It is an achievement. If you had a high position, you would do everything in your power to keep it. If you knew that you and your wife had but one more day of life to live, you would put aside everything to make that day beautiful."

So would I speak to husbands and wives somehow to make them realize that they must forgo their childish dreams and fantasies, must cease making each other miserable because of impossible expectations, must understand that all of human experience is adjustment and compromise. Why should we human beings expect to find perfection in life? Science teaches us that the whole universe is in process of evolution. There is great waste, futility, error in all of nature. Throughout billions of years this planet has been making countless experiments, always striving for the better. The world did not come perfect from the hand of God; it moves through struggle, trial and failure from the less adequate to the more adequate, from the less sensitive to the more sensitive, from blind matter to the dreaming mind. We who are part of this revolutionary process should not expect to be free of the laws which apply to stardust and ocean depths. In love and in marriage we fall to rise again. As children of an evolutionary universe, we should anticipate failure and disappointment, as well as success and achievement. This is the universal law of life. Why indeed should we alone be privileged to experience good and not evil, joy and not pain, success and not failure? No, our expectations have been pitched too high. This is the source of our unhappiness and our frustration. A wise rule for life would be to expect toil and disillusionment, and to be radiantly surprised at every good thing, every sign of affection, every token of devotion which you encounter in your journey from horizon to horizon, from east to west.

I have spoken of a few of the obstacles to happiness in marriage. What are some of the aids to that happiness, the rules and the ingredients for success? What are the designs for the pattern of marital joy? Man has four basic requirements—physiological adjustment, psychological tolerance, sociological security, and religious integration. These four needs of man symbolize to me four of the basic designs for happiness in marriage and in love.

The first is the acceptance of the physical basis of marriage. Certainly our physical desires bring pain as well as joy. They are like earthquake and dynamite; badly handled, they can bring much unhappiness. Any desire of man misused and abused brings suffering. Judaism has always made of our desires potential sacraments which through discipline and control and wise usage can be instruments to great and noble values. The body is an instrument leading to intrinsic values, the values of home and children, of family and society. Judaism has never gone to the extreme found in some other religions, of teaching that marriage is a concession to human weakness, a surrender to evil temptation. It was Greek thought that separated body and soul and created the tragic dualism that led to the ideal of celibacy in Christianity. In Judaism celibacy was opposed and marriage was exalted because body and spirit were regarded as an interwoven unity. Judaism emphasized the necessity, not of the denial of the flesh for the sake of the spirit, and not of the exaltation of the flesh in contempt of the spirit, but of the sanctification of the flesh by the spirit.

The rabbis proclaimed that without the desires of the body no man would build a house, or marry a wife. Without the body there is no knowledge, no life, and no performance of mitzvoth (good deeds). To Hillel the body was for this reason a sanctuary.

This has been the healthy-minded attitude of Israel, and for this reason in traditional Judaism there has been little of the self-torture and self-torment, the tragic guilt feelings, which have ruined so many lives in Western society. "God," we said, "has given us bodies as well as souls, and if we use both of them wisely, justly, reverently, we are serving best the purposes of our Creator." Much of modern marriage has been unhappy because this balanced perspective of Judaism was not the dominating tradition in the Western world. There has been a quick transition in the twentieth century from Victorian prudishness to anti-Victorian libertinism. The pendulum swung too far from the ideal of repression to the ideal of expression. Repression caused all kinds of neuroses; expression has brought all kinds of excesses. We need both freedom and discipline, structure and spontaneity. Marriage gives us the structure, the permanence, the abiding house for our feelings, and within that structure we can find expression for our basic needs, physical and spiritual. The first rule of happiness is to recognize that men and women should express themselves, their yearnings, their passions, their hopes within the circle of each other. Monogamy, Judaism teaches, is the ideal pattern of marriage because no matter how liberal men and women may think they are in theory, in reality they are emotionally limited and are unable to share the one that they love with another person. Any experienced rabbi or psychiatrist comes to the conclusion that human experience proves the validity of monogamy.

The first design for personal happiness in marriage, then, is to accept yourself as a human being with all the limitations and imperfections—and also with the possibilities—which the term "human being" implies. You are not a pure spirit, an angel floating disembodied in the air; you are an animal organism endowed with certain capacities for spiritual achievement. The basic rule for wisdom in this sphere, as in any other, is to accept yourself, to realize that marriage has been ordained by divinity and by society as a wonderful institution whereby men and women can find completion in each other. To be ashamed of the body, to turn away in repugnance from human love, to torment oneself with feelings of guilt at the expression of one's yearnings in marriage, is to blaspheme the Creator of the universe who has endowed man with body as well as with soul as the instruments of

151

creation. Neither the denial of the body, nor the glorification of the body, but its sanctification through and by the spirit of love, of devotion and holiness, is implicit in this endowment.

The second great design for personal happiness in marriage is the achievement of compatibility. By this I mean the art of getting along with one another. Compatibility is, of course, desirable in all human relationships, but has particular urgency between husband and wife. It is not achieved in a moment or in a year; it is a task for a lifetime, and even a lifetime may be too short for a husband and wife to achieve complete adjustment to each other.

Modern psychology indicates to us how subtle and complicated is this problem of compatibility. We have to understand many new truths in this realm. When we marry, we become united not merely with a particular adult girl or man, but with the whole process of the bride or the bridegroom. What Alfred North Whitehead indicated in his *Process and Reality* applies to us as individuals. We are not merely our present; we are also our past and our future. We should remember, as it has been well said, that although your bride is twenty-two years old, you are really marrying her childhood in great part, and the young woman who thinks she is marrying the successful young businessman is in a deeper sense marrying as well his feelings, his experiences, his attitudes as they were established at the age of four or five, when he may have been pampered by an oversolicitous parent or emotionally starved by a too-neglectful parent. The infant is the father to the child; the child is the father to the man. The boy is indeed the first edition of the husband; the girl is the first edition of the wife. Therefore, many of the problems which occur in marriage occur not on the adult level but on the childhood level. Many husbands vacillate between trying to act the role of parent to the wife and also at the other extreme act the role of child to the wife. The same thing is true with regard to the wife. Compatibility is achieved when each understands the whole life story of the other, recognizes that there are always vestigial remains of puberty and adolescence and of the unhappy experiences of infancy. When husband and wife cease trying to play the role of child or of parent to each other, when they recognize that many of their quarrels come from immature jealousies and childish angers, then only do they establish a mature compatibility. Adult life means the surrender of fantasies and dreams and patterns which were perfectly normal in babyhood, but which are out of place in marital maturity. Most people maintain within themselves an enormous standing army to defend themselves against straw men, against ghosts. The energy that is squandered by a husband or a wife in protecting himself or herself against childish fears, jealousies, selfishness, could solve almost all the real problems which are the lot of every couple.

Much incompatibility could be eliminated if we would become psychically tolerant of each other. Socrates' phrase *Know thyself,* Spinoza's memorable admonition, *Do not condemn and do not judge, but understand*—both apply profoundly to the marriage relationship. In our childhood and youth each one of us identifies with some adult. It may be father or mother. We carry this identification into our mature experience. Many of the quarrels of marriage come from the fact that we still are playing a role, either that of the shielded child or the all-dominant, possessive father. As soon as we are aware of the origin of our incompatibility, and see that our present attitudes have nothing to do with the world in which we now live, but are mere remnants of a not wholly discarded past, we begin to discover the

153

road to compatibility as adults. Stop being a baby! Stop being an adolescent! are two admonitions that could, if they were heeded, save many a marriage from ruin. Psychological happiness in marriage is achieved when we become tolerant of each other and recognize that each of us is inevitably a process in a reality, that there are earlier selves bound up in our ego, and that we must distinguish between our childish self and our adult self. On this road lies psychic happiness.

The third design for personal happiness is security. This security can be found within the new social group. Let there be no mistake about this. When a young man and a young woman marry, they are establishing a new society, a society consisting of two members. This is the smallest social group in all the world, but in some respects the most important. The members of that group are the most interdependent of all because marriage deals with every layer of the personality. When we are members of a family or a society or a club or a lodge, we are related to other members only by one or two aspects of our beings. In marriage, we are compelled to say "yes" to both the agreeable and disagreeable qualities of our partners, to recognize that we share all experiences together. Insecurity in this group leads to the greatest unhappiness. Security in marriage, on the other hand, means that there is some haven where a person feels accepted and feels reassured of his worth. A lack of truthfulness, the practice of deception in any way, shatters the very ground upon which husband and wife stand and destroys that fundamental design which is psychic security. Ofttimes men and women keep silent and refuse to confide in each other. That lack of confidence itself helps to wither and to destroy love; it creates ever greater chasms between the partners in the marriage relationship. The security that marriage requires can be achieved in this little group only if these requirements are met. In the first place, each one should adapt himself as much as possible to the needs of the other, to the physical, social and spiritual requirements of his beloved. In the second place, there should be a sufficient freedom of movement, enough friendships outside the circle of marriage, to prevent the suffocation of the marriage itself. In the third place, the new group should be given priority over all previous groups. The husband and the wife should know that all previous loyalties are now secondary to the loyalty within the circle of their marriage. This is very simple to remember.

A few years ago, a young couple in another city, whom I had come to admire very much, came to see me. They told me that they were on the brink of divorce. I asked the reason. It turned out that in spite of the fact that he was a brilliant young doctor and she was a gifted artist, they were carrying with them primal loyalties to the families from which they had emerged. He was an only child who had been pampered and idolized; she was one of a number of children and expected him to feel as close to her brothers and sisters as she felt; he, however, wanted all of her love reserved for him. I pointed out that they had created a new society when they married. They must not permit any extraneous tensions upon their relationship. Happily, they listened to the advice given them, realized that they must understand not only the present but also the past of each other's experience, and that their first and primal loyalty was to the new little group which they had fashioned.

Security in marriage, then, means also willingness to cut the cord which binds children to parents and makes them dependent upon father and mother. It means that husband and wife will rely upon each other's wisdom, love, and understanding, and will not seek support, advice, or guidance outside the magic circle of love. Man and woman in marriage must have the security of knowing that in hours of crisis it literally means two against the world. The little social group made up of husband and wife can give each of the partners a sense of at-homeness, of belonging, a safety which neither can obtain alone. Certainly some freedom must be sacrificed for the sake of marriage, but marriage can become so important a part of life that the goals of one partner become to a high degree the other's goals. A certain amount of freedom has to be given up as a condition of membership in any group. But what glorious compensation comes from the "we" feeling: the sense of mutual strength, devotion, sacrifice, escape from loneliness, trust and confidence, consideration of each other's needs and desires, the rights to one's individuality and separate interests as well as mutual interests; in other words, sufficient freedom of movement within the circle of marriage, the primacy of the marriage group above all other groups—family or religion or nation. These are the means by which the security of marriage is achieved.

In other words, marriage is the establishment of a group where we can find our true social security. This is what makes infidelity so great a wrong. It removes the ground from under one's feet. Marriage really is the creation of an entirely new allegiance. It is taking out citizenship papers, being naturalized in the state of matrimony. When two young people sanctify themselves in marriage, they really should understand that they are forswearing all the old allegiances which had prior claims on them. This does not mean that they should not love and respect father and mother or family. A man who becomes a naturalized citizen of the United States may well retain certain bonds of affection for the culture of his first homeland; but just as we insist that a new citizen of this land shall have no dual allegiances, so in marriage there should be that insistence. There must be no dual allegiances. There must be a basic loyalty to the new society, the country of the soul where love rules. It is indeed true that there is a certain clannishness and exclusiveness in marriage. It is inevitable that this should be so. Husband and wife should retain a normal interest in other people, in their friends, in their dear ones, but they should recognize that their fundamental loyalty is to each other. To be a citizen in this little country of marriage means that each one has duties and each one has rights, but that as long as life itself exists the spiritual flag of that new land should never be lowered into the dust. That symbol of security, of confidence, and of mutual trust should never be destroyed by the weapons of the outer world. Each happy marriage is the creation of a new society. Enough happy marriages in the world would really create an international society, a league of spiritual nations where true peace and justice could be found.

The fourth design I see as necessary for personal happiness in marriage comes through religious aspiration. Loyalty to one another does not mean that husband and wife should shut themselves off from the larger universe of mankind. The greater the security within the circle of marriage, the more the husband and wife should be challenged to give of themselves to the eternal purposes spoken of by religion. We human beings are strange creatures in a strange universe. We are not put here to be mere clods of earth, unfeeling rock and stone; we are to be fighters for ends, seekers of goals, achievers of great purposes. The religious doctrine that Judaism teaches is that this is a world where man is not merely to receive but to give, to create value as well as to accept it. Whenever two happy people are inspired to concern themselves with the needs and hopes of mankind, to struggle for an increase in national righteousness, in international decency and honor, there we have a religious way of life. Marriage is never happy when it becomes ingrown, circumscribed, egocentric. It is creative and joyous when two people with all their mutual understanding and love add to the life-giving forces in the universe and become partners with divinity in making the world nobler, freer, lovelier for those who are yet to be born. If God is conceived as the power that sustains life and conserves value, then man and woman, taken out of the narrow sphere of selfish interest and inspired to identify themselves with the larger causes of human goodness, are truly His agents on earth. A marriage can find its highest happiness when husband and wife devote themselves to the service of humanity and the search for divinity. Religion takes marriage out of itself and gives it eternal purpose.

These, then, are the four designs for personal happiness in marriage. First, learn to accept yourself and your physical desires with natural piety; second, understand that you are a psychological person, a union of past and present and future; third, realize that in marriage you become a citizen of a new republic, the democracy of matrimony, to which spiritual state you must give your primary loyalty so that through it you may find your unshaken security. And, finally, visualize your marriage as a religious means to a religious end, the privilege given to you and your partner together to add to life's possibilities and glories, and thus to become joint co-workers with deity.

There are many other designs which could be mentioned for personal happiness. The ability to rise above jealousy, to conquer pettiness of mind and narrowness of spirit, the willingness to forgive and to overlook, the capacity to be generous as well

158

as wise in matters of money, the display of courtesy, attentiveness and charm after marriage as well as before—all these play their indubitable roles in making for success in this difficult art.

A successful marriage is not a miraculous gift; it is a human achievement. There can be no universal rules applicable to each individual situation. Happiness has something of a mystic quality about it. It is ineffable and indescribable, yet if men and women are willing to learn wisdom from the experience of the human race, they will know that marriage can be made radiant. Each husband and each wife is like a sculptor working in precious marble and making it come alive; or to use a metaphor, marriage is the ploughing of soil, sometimes rocky, sometimes rich. The harvest we garner only at the end of days. Those of us who have this gift of marriage should treasure it well.

Too often we take for granted the blessings which are ours. Life is barren enough, friendships are few enough, honor and power and achievement fade away, but love abides and remains. It can be at the end of life even as in the beginning of life. If we will it so, we can graduate from the university of marriage at death "summa cum laude." Mistakes we will make. This is the price we pay for living. If the mistakes become too serious and too depressing, let us go to some wise doctor, some sympathetic counselor, some experienced minister. There is no disgrace in consulting experts. We do not wait until disease destroys our health before consulting a physician. We should not wait until misunderstanding destroys our marriage and often needlessly brings us to desolation and loneliness, before we seek counsel, guidance, and a new path. The greatest insight we can have is the insight into our own limitations, to recognize that we are both free and determined, that we can take our normal risks and face our normal problems with hope and confidence. No human mistake is irrevocable and no matter what happens, we can try again. Other people have succeeded; other personalities have developed. Other beautiful marriages have been realized. If we will it so, a creative partnership can be ours throughout the changing years. We can never hope to escape problems, troubles, disappointments within the circle of home as within the circle of the world at large, but if we tend the soil and watch the growing plant yielding its fruit we can say with Browning: "The best is yet to be, the last of life, for which the first was made."

HONOR THY SON AND THY DAUGHTER

One of the great commandments of Judaism is "Honor thy father and thy mother that thy days may be long upon the land which the Lord thy God giveth thee."

In Judaism, this famous commandment became a cornerstone of group life. The rabbis dwelt upon reverence of parents as essential to the survival and the strength of Israel. How beautiful are some of the passages from the Midrash and the Talmud: "Every time a man honors his father and his mother, the Holy One, blessed be He, says 'I shall reward them as though I had dwelt among them and they had honored Me.'" The love of a son for his mother is unforgettably phrased in the sentence of Rabbi Joseph, who, when he heard the sound of his mother's footsteps, called out, "I shall rise before the Divine Presence that is coming."

It is a well-ingrained doctrine in Judaism—and through Judaism it has been woven into the moral fabric of the rest of the world—that reverence for parents is the indispensable ingredient in a stable and serene family life. Nor is this in any way surprising. Honoring father and mother is quite natural, since they constitute our first real contacts with the world. It is the voice of the mother that is the first melody of love heard by a child's ears. It is the strong and seemingly omnipotent father who gives the infant his first intimations of strength and competence and wisdom. Our parents are indeed our first models. It is no exaggeration at all to say that there are multitudes of men and women who are deaf today to the melody of affection and security and serenity in the world because they never heard that melody sung by the mother. There are millions of people walking the streets of life who are blind to goodness, truth, and beauty because their fathers before them had no vision and communicated no vision to the next generation. It is the voice of a mother and the voice of a father that can make us forever deaf to the music of life or, if we are fortunate, can open the inner ear of our souls to all of the rhythms and harmonies of existence.

Some parents are genuine heroes and heroines, worthy patterns to follow. Others just give the appearance of being heroic. In actuality their temperaments, their moods, their characters can make them villains in the drama of their children's existence, and the evil that they do indeed lives after them in the twisted and distorted outlook, the inner misery, the psychic phobias and fears of their offspring.

Maimonides, the greatest of the Jewish philosophers, had some very interesting and important truths to teach our generation about parents and children. As a good Jew he believed in the importance of the commandment "Honor thy father and thy mother," but he made it very clear that this love in a sense should be conditional: "Honor thy father and mother provided they deserve and merit honor." Maimonides understood that there are some parents who believe that they can demand everything of their children, even though they have given little to them. Parents, he thought, should be very considerate and forgiving of the shortcomings of their children, understanding the inner heart of their son and daughter. This great Jewish teacher went so far as to maintain that while we owe infinitely much to our forebears and should always bestow love and concern upon those who have brought us into the world and given us our first acquaintanceship with the world, nevertheless this law also has its exceptions. He maintained that the moral law itself can become immoral in a certain sense if it is carried to an extreme. For example, children should not destroy their lives and health or their children's lives and health for the sake of parents who are overdemanding or whose mental condition is such that the family life is clouded and darkened without any real help being given to the afflicted one. Maimonides says, "If parents cannot really be helped by their children, then let provision be made for their care and help by experts, by doctors and nurses." We should honor our parents and love them, but not to the point of destroying needlessly and fruitlessly our own lives and the lives of those who come after us. How desperately is this wisdom of Maimonides needed in our own day!

I would not wish to give a false impression. In many households the relationship between parents and children is not a problem, but rather a solution. There is an intuitive warmth, a shared joy, a mutual respect, which make of life something radiant and lovely and profoundly meaningful. The human race would not have survived if there had not been in every part of the world mothers and fathers without instruction in the subtleties of psychology and of child education who knew, out of their abundance of love, how to give strength and security and a deep trustfulness in the glory of existence. We Jews certainly know that in our tradition the home has been an altar, and fathers and mothers have been high priests and high priestesses, ministering at that altar, bestowing the gifts of idealism and laughter and learning and deep psychic fulfillment upon the children with whom they were blessed. Oh, it is a great mistake to think of the family only as a problem, as do so many sociologists and psychologists today! The family at its best is fulfillment, not frustration.

However, it is quite true that in our restless modern civilization the family reveals many splits and partitions in its essential unity. Gone indeed are the frontier days in this land, when generations of one family were bound together by tilling the same soil, living and finding happiness in the same strong house built by the muscles and the sweat and the toil of fathers and sons. Gone is the family pattern of self-sufficiency, with its simplicity, its mutuality, and its emotional unity. Ours is a very complex age, and there is infinitely more frustration for fathers and mothers going out into the world of the market place, feeling themselves cogs in an endless machine, fatigued and unsatisfied in their quest for status, never knowing the kind of economic and social security which would enable them to be well-integrated patterns for their children. They go to work tired and they come home tired. There is a marathon race going on, among rich and poor, for more power, more prestige, with little time for the slow growth of comradeship between the older and the younger generations. The tempo is swift. The clamor is shattering. Values are distorted. The blossoms of family solidarity, understanding and mutual love cannot grow in the hothouse of our neurotic, uncertain, confused and frightened epoch.

It is more difficult to be a parent in this age than it was in the simpler civilizations of yore. As a result, fathers and mothers, exposed to all the veering winds of doctrine, listening to conflicting counsel, are often like the centipede, that hundred-legged creature who, when he was asked how he walked, just did not know which leg he began with. With all the multiplicity of voices shouting in the ears of parents today, it is no wonder that many fathers and mothers are afraid to take any stand, are anxious about any step, concerned about the impact of this deed or that decision upon the mental or physical well-being of a son or a daughter. The parent-child relationship in our age is compounded of far more elements of confusion and of conflict than in any previous century. Yet unless we achieve a new clarity about the relationship between parents and children, we might as well forget our hope of a peaceful society and a better future for humanity. The home is the laboratory, and the family is the test tube in which we grow the cultures of health or of disease; many a man today is the carrier of infection to his whole society because he was subtly contaminated (and poisoned) in his childhood; many a woman becomes a frustrating, denying, and miserably unhappy mother who places the burden of futility and distraction upon her children's shoulders just because she herself never received the kind of understanding, affection and warmth that she required in her early years.

I believe, therefore, that we need today not only the commandment "Honor thy father and thy mother," but also another commandment: "Honor thy son and thy daughter." Certainly this law is by no means well established in the minds of parents who believe that they are "sacrificing everything" for their children. It probably will come as a surprise to many parents that with the best intentions in the world they are often actually damaging, distorting, dishonoring their children. Oh,

I can anticipate vigorous disagreement with this point of view: "Why, parents are too lenient with their children. The younger generation is running wild. What they need is the stern rod of discipline." My answer is: If the coming generation is in danger, and all signs show that this is so, the reason is directly traceable to the fact that many American fathers and mothers have not sufficiently understood the profound and inescapable necessity of "honoring" their sons and their daughters.

"To honor" is an expression carrying with it almost forgotten overtones of unconditional love, respect for personality, and tolerance for inevitable human shortcomings. We all of us have been taught by our religions and by our Western culture to feel terribly guilty if we do not accord these signs of devotion to our parents; but on the other hand, parents, too, rarely feel an equal obligation to manifest this sort of honor for their offspring. Americans lead the world in giving clothes, food, amusement, education to their boys and girls, but somewhere and somehow the concept of honoring their children has been pitiably left out.

"Honor thy son and thy daughter." This, it seems to me, is the great goal of familial relationships. Parents should strive to make of the home a little democracy—a democracy in which the father and the mother are the leaders and the children in many respects the followers, but in which all have an opportunity of expressing their opinions, giving voice to their desires, and having the laws of that little democracy reviewed from time to time, revised, changed, and brought up to date. In the home, if anywhere, the ideal of the Golden Mean should be established—the mean between extremes. There should be a balance in family relationships between frustration and fulfillment, between discipline and devotion.

Children do need to be frustrated in many of their imperious wishes and desires. They have to learn early that life does not bestow upon them the unattainable moons of their yearning, that life at times is hard, and that the world is not created to be the servant of their whims. At the same time every family should have within it great areas of fulfillment, not only in laws but in love. What I mean by the establishment of a little democracy in the family circle is that though the parents should be recognized as leaders, it should nevertheless also be recognized that the children have rights as well as duties.

Throughout the ages religion has created an enormous Bill of Rights for parents. Now has come the time when we have to write a Bill of Rights for children as well. In the home at its best we should have a system of checks and balances, a democracy that avoids the extreme on the one hand of tyranny, where the father plays the role of dictator—or the mother stars in the drama as the omnipotent ruler—or on the other hand an extreme of anarchy in which there are no laws, no rules, no accepted code of behavior or discipline. Sons and daughters cannot develop their fullest potentialities in either a despotism or an anarchy. They will emerge from the walls of the family sanctuary twisted and distorted in some fashion or other if they have been compelled to submit to the decrees of a father or a mother tyrant, or, on the other hand, if they have received from the parental atmosphere no firmness, no justifiable frustration, but only overindulgence or overprotection that ill prepares them for the genuine realities of the world of men and of women.

The goals as I see them, then, are the establishment of a democracy in the home, and in this little republic of the family, parents must recognize that their sons and daughters are personalities in their own right, not mere pawns on a chessboard of parental ambition or vanity. What a great liberation will come to the world when fathers and mothers realize that they do not own their children merely by virtue of the biological accident of birth, and when they come to see that the little infant or the growing boy or the adolescent daughter possesses the inalienable rights given to every human soul by God, and not merely the specific rights bestowed by the omniscient and all-powerful parent. The tragedy which is too little recognized in our age is that in this acquisitive society some fathers and mothers make their children their possessions; if they do not possess enough stocks or bonds or material things in the world of prestige, they often attempt to make their offspring their compensation for failure or disappointment in the great race of life, and look to their sons and daughters to compensate them for all the blocks and obstacles in their quest for ego-satisfaction.

If a home is to be a democracy, the children have to be respected as personalities in their own right and a climate has to be fashioned for them—a climate of consistency and of predictability. What do I mean by this? I mean that there should be a dependable emotional atmosphere in which the child is raised. It should be a temperate zone. A child cannot stand a parental environment which is 98 degrees in the shade of love one hour and 20 degrees below zero of rejection the next hour. Make no mistake about it: boys and girls seek discipline as well as devotion, firmness as well as love; but the firmness should be well defined and mutually understood and should not be merely the expression of an angry mood or an irrational caprice. Predictability and probability are now great words in science, for without them no mastery of physical nature is possible. Well, boys and girls depend on predictability in the attitudes of their parents, just as much as the chemist depends on other natural laws in his laboratory. I do not mean to suggest that fathers and mothers should go around taking their own and their children's emotional temperatures all the time. Occasional outbursts of parental anger or fits of moodiness are both normal, and are relatively unimportant so long as the boys and girls have been given an unwavering sense of emotional security and know with all their hearts that they are loved, wanted and respected. A certain stability on the part of parents is obligatory, a consistency which will make possible the beginning of a democracy in the home.

Our goal, then, is that of truly honoring our sons and our daughters and so creating a genuine democracy in the sanctuary of the home. But as we look at the world we certainly find many deviations from that goal—deviations that are ultimately responsible for much of the misery and unhappiness of human life. World literature, for example, abounds in illustrations of lives ruined by the false and ultimately destructive attitudes of fathers and mothers toward their offspring. One remarkable illustration, for example, is found in Shakespeare's *Coriolanus*. In this play the central character of the tragedy, a great Roman soldier, has been molded and shaped by his mother, that stern, austere, demanding, dictatorial Roman matron, into the arrogant egoist who brought misery to himself and to Rome. There are other examples: Balzac rejected in childhood by his greedy and self-pitying mother, Dostoevski twisted into inner loneliness by his antisocial and essentially insecure doctor-father, George Sand, made incapable of knowing true feminine love because her domineering grandmother, the real mother-figure in her life, always wanted her to be a boy and dressed her as a boy.

We see that fathers and mothers dishonor their sons and daughters consciously or unconsciously, not only in literature but also in real life. Now, it is quite true that cruelty is often quite unconscious, and the real damage to the children takes place in disguised forms and on levels that are not even remotely realized by the parents. How common, for example, is the following situation in our contemporary industrial society. A father, thwarted and frustrated in a very dull job, hating the work by which he has to earn his bread and unable to find relief for the tensions that accumulate in his routine work, takes out his feeling of defeat subtly or overtly upon his children. They must have perfect manners, they must obey instantly and implicitly, they must be subject to him who, poor man, is elsewhere so subjugated by others. I am certain that this father often imagines himself to be a model parent doing what he does in the name of discipline, for the good of his children. The truth of the matter, deep beneath the surface, is that he is visiting upon his children all the subtle degradations that are visited upon him in his workaday world. More often than we suspect, a child becomes a whipping boy, a scapegoat for the misery and the unhappiness of the parent. It is just too bad that there are no recognized laws protecting children from the subtle scapegoatism of the home. We do have laws in the United States against making scapegoats out of minority groups. Well, children are often in the position of minority groups in the society of the home. Many are the lynching parties that occur in that little society. The father may release enormous aggression by taking out his frustration upon his helpless child; but this is costly therapy indeed!

There are other ways in which a parent dishonors his child. A woman, for example, who has always wanted to become a singer and has dreamed of captivating a great audience at the Metropolitan Opera House, fails to attain her ambition, marries and brings into the world a lovely daughter. From babyhood that child is twisted, shaped, and molded into the role of singer. The mother, whether she knows it or not, is determined to get her second chance out of life by driving her daughter to become the triumphant opera star that she had once dreamed of becoming. No matter if the girl herself fails to possess the talent or the desire to achieve artistic preeminence; often she just is not consulted. She is a victim placed upon the sacrificial altar of her mother's ambition.

A very vivid example of parental dictatorship once came to my attention in a letter from a man in the Middle West—a man of thirty—who suffered from deep depression and a sense of haunting failure. When I realized that his need was very deep, I arranged for a meeting. I learned that he was the typical product of a home that had never recognized the right to self-determination on the part of children as they grow and mature. His father, quite successful as a shoe manufacturer, had forced this sensitive, artistic lad to follow in his mercantile footsteps. Raised in a pious Christian home and conditioned by the Biblical commandment, the young man had obeyed his father, but at what a cost! He was lost in an assembly line of shoes when he really wanted to be among the paint brushes and easels of the studio. Whether he would have become a great artist if the father had truly honored his son's talents is irrelevant; the boy would at least have become a happier, better-adjusted human being.

How many times do we not see fathers attempting to make of their sons the elongated shadows of their own life goals; how many mothers who transform their children into display pieces in the drawing room of their vanity.

These forms of dishonoring the young soul are not always obvious to the parent, to the child, or to anyone but the most penetrating outside observer. Yet the damage is being done nevertheless.

How can the tragic errors that reveal themselves in such cases as those of Balzac, Dostoevski, and George Sand, and such other tragic mistakes in the relationships between parents and children as we have noted, be avoided? How can parents learn truly "to honor their sons and their daughters"? It seems to me that the most important truth that can be acquired by the builders of the home should be that flexible strategy is requisite on the part of fathers and mothers toward their sons and daughters, and that in each stage of the child's development a new approach is necessary. What worked beautifully in infancy certainly will not work in puberty or in adolescence. Some parents who are wonderful with infants—cooing, loving, anticipating the baby's every wish—seem to fall short when the child leaves the nursery. Such fathers and mothers really yearn to prolong the stage of helpesss dependence, overprotecting their offspring, producing quite frequently the coddled and spoiled darling who is never quite able to come to terms with mature reality. Likewise, when their sons or daughters enter the strange grove of adolescence, some parents are completely bewildered. The techniques that worked in infancy or even in early childhood are no longer valuable; indeed they may prove harmful.

Parenthood is the most demanding career of all, perhaps, and flexibility is even more important in this career than in the business world—flexibility in accordance with the new needs of the growing personality of the boy or girl. It is often mystifying to me to see how many fathers and mothers who are quite anxious to keep up-to-date in fashion, in social relationships, in their acquaintance with the newest books and the newest music, in their business techniques or their professional competence, are so out-of-date in dealing with their own flesh and blood. The same master of an industrial empire who obtains the newest patents and has on his staff of advisers the greatest experts to tell him of new laws that have been passed that affect his particular enterprise—this man, who is so notably ahead of his field in sensing the pulse of the present and even of the future, acts toward his grown daughter as though she were, still, emotionally speaking, a pink-and-white baby in a crib, rather than a quite competent and hungry-for-independence young woman. The very lawyer or doctor or scientist who would be ashamed of remaining uninformed about the latest developments in his particular field is quite oblivious to the fact that as a parent he is static and rigid, fixed on some early pattern that is tragically out of date for the true development of his boy's or girl's personality.

This same rigidity and inflexibility are often evident in mothers. A fashionable lady who would rather be found dead than wearing last year's hat or last year's dress may actually wear last decade's hat and dress, psychologically speaking, in her relationship to son and to daughter. Is there a greater error or a greater source of human misery than inflexibility and rigidity on the part of a mother and father who think that because they have dealt adequately with their child as an infant and have protected and shielded and advised him and brought him through the perilous shoals of childhood diseases, they are therefore quite able to apply the same technique to the lad in puberty (and the girl in adolescence)? No wonder there are so many emotional cripples and maladjusted neurotics in the United States today. They are the products of homes where the father and the mother proved failures as parents because of their archaic attitudes, because of their failure to recognize that motherhood and fatherhood are processes, not static conditions. They have not taken account of the fact that at different stages of development boys and girls require absolutely different approaches. The baby needs love, the child in puberty more than anything else

172

needs security, and the adolescent needs permission to grow more independent of parental advice, guidance and domination.

This, too, should not be too difficult to understand. In our relationship to our parents we adopt a flexible attitude and a changing strategy. When we are little children, we think of our fathers and mothers as powerful, dominant, strong, almost omnipotent, and we look to them for everything. And then as we grow up, if we are successful in our relationship with fathers and mothers, we begin to look upon them as comrades, as good companions; and then as they grow old and enter the twilight period of their existence, we deal with them not as we dealt with them when we were little children—we deal with them as dependent, lovable, revered elders who need us and depend upon us just as long ago we depended upon them. We *change* in our attitude toward our parents with the different epochs of life. The analogous truth should be applied by parents dealing with their children. Let us be far more worried about being out-of-date in our handling of the deep inner needs of our boys and girls than about our mastery of the latest technique in law or business or medicine, or the acquisition of the most fashionable dress or suit or hair style of the moment. Let us always be concerned with that which is appropriate in each stage of our child's evolution. A baby that is given independence is just as tragic a figure as an adolescent who is never given independence. The infant needs to be showered with love. The adolescent needs to be given freedom from an over-demanding protection.

I am thinking of the case of a friend—Dorothy—who, when she was a little child, suffered from a very severe mastoid infection. Her parents were understandably concerned, and when Dorothy recovered, she was surrounded on all sides not only by her parents but also by her grandparents and aunts with an atmosphere of love and attention. She grew up into a healthy young girl, but in her family's eyes she was still the "delicate" Dorothy, never quite strong enough to take her place among her classmates at school. This attitude continued through puberty and into adolescence. Her mother made her constantly aware of the danger of germs and of colds; the world began to be populated for her with enemies called microbes, and she developed into a hypochondriacal individual, in spite of the fact that she had never had any major illness since that childhood infection. She is now a rather isolated, lonely woman; she has never married, but has gone from doctor to doctor, a burden to herself and to those who know her, her real possibilities for creative happiness ruined by parental folly. This may seem like an extreme case, but it can be duplicated again and again and again when parents have allowed themselves to be fixated upon one level of their child's problem and their child's development.

Far wiser are the fathers and mothers who refuse to coddle their children, who train them to take the normal risks of life as part of the business of living in a rather risky universe. A young boy who, though rather thin and wiry, has a great desire for athletic competition, and becomes a quarterback on his high school football team even though his parents are afraid that he might get some bones broken in the contest, will receive from the example of his father and mother a sense of self-reliance and courage and the knowledge that in the game of life many bones may be broken, both physical and spiritual, and yet can be healed again.

In the first place, give your child unconditional love. This is a basic law for the family pattern. Parents think that they are giving love to their children when, as a matter of fact, they are showing rejection or hostility or disappointment, all wearing the disguises of love. One of the great dangers in American civilization is that fathers and mothers trained in this highly competitive society try to "keep up with the Joneses," try to win higher and higher places on the ladder of success; such parents make their children feel that their love is conditional. Their behavior implies: "*If* you get a good report card, *if* you make the honor roll, *if* you show yourself to be the prettiest, the best-behaved, the ablest, the wisest, the strongest in your schoolroom, then you will receive all the emoluments of affection. But if, on the other hand, you do not make me proud of you, if you disappoint me, then I will reject you, if not overtly, then in some hidden fashion." I say that this is the greatest crime that can be perpetrated upon a child; to be given a sense of his own worthlessness, his valuelessness—and consequently a sense of the futility of life. Unconditional love is the first law of honoring your son and your daughter.

The second law of honoring your son and your daughter is the law of acceptance. Accept your child not only for what he is, and incidentally for what he can become, but accept him also in the realm of nature. Understand that he is equipped with many characteristics that come from our common universal animal ancestors, that your son or daughter possesses instincts and impulses that are not purely angelic. Do not become tense and temperamental about these casual and unimportant manifestations of the animal aspects of your child's nature. Many fathers and mothers ruthlessly punish any manifestation of the fact that their child, like every other person in the world, is possessed of a body as well as of a soul. This punishment is ofttimes unconscious self-punishment, fear on the part of the father or the mother of some unacknowledged impulse or instinct not worked out in his own childhood. I say that if you want really to honor your children, take them for granted as partly animal and partly angelic and wholly human. Do not be surprised or horrified at the outcropping of erotic impulses which will afterward be disciplined into quite acceptable pathways and patterns of moral, decent and creative marital fulfillment. Do not warp and twist and torment your child's whole life because he happens to have been endowed by God with flesh as well as with mind and spirit, and do not take the passing impulse or the fantasy of the moment as a permanent, unchangeable character trait. Look upon your child as a tree that grows, dropping many old leaves of unacceptable aggression and hostility and eroticism, and that will, through wise love and wise acceptance, one day put on the wonderful new foliage of mature fulfillment, physical and spiritual.

I would say that the third basic law for honor of son and daughter is that of respect. Respect your child for what he is and for what he wants to become. Give your children permission to grow up and become mature, independent men and women in their own right. In dealing with your adolescent son or daughter, gradually achieve the wisdom of renunciation described with brilliant simplicity by Carl Sandburg: "Loosen your hand, let go, and say goodbye." This is perhaps the most misunderstood and the most difficult law of all. Parents often think that they are respecting the pattern of their son or their daughter, but all that they are doing is trying to force their offspring into their own mold.

It takes genuine renunciation on the part of parents to allow their children the sovereign rights of maturity and independence, and yet that is the meaning of truly unselfish love. Many a mother thinks that she loves her son, yet she keeps the silver cord uncut, subtly dominating his emotional existence even after marriage as she refuses to allow her boy to establish his own

176

little republic of love and family. Many a father just cannot make peace with the fact that his boy, having become a young man, is no longer dependent upon his advice and is no longer subject to his whims and his decrees. Literature abounds in tragic stories of parents who have never permitted the children to be free of the tether of familial tyranny.

It takes real greatness for a father and a mother to cut the cord of dependence for their children, to realize that after all the investment of time, energy, sacrifice and suffering, the son or the daughter may grow distant, may feel remote, may act at times like a stranger. This, too, is part of the infinite burden of existence; but boys and girls in adolescence and in early maturity should be given the opportunity to choose their way of life without dictatorship from any parental throne. Freedom is something more than the right to a ballot; it is something more than a political arrangement. Freedom is also the choice of an individual of the way that he wants to live his life, to find his fulfillment; and that choice should be granted ungrudgingly by parents to their offspring, so long as the way of life chosen is decent and its pattern of fulfillment satisfying and enriching.

I am thinking now of a good friend of mine in the Middle West who really honored his son's personality. The father is a distinguished lawyer; he had long dreamed that his firstborn would become a member of his law firm. However, the boy was utterly bored with abstract legal concepts but powerfully fascinated by engines and machines. His own idea of paradise was to work in a garage, and from his high school days he was to be found after school amid the oil and steel of his mechanical heaven. His deeply understanding father renounced his own cherished ambition for his son, encouraged him to follow his mechanical bent, to train himself in that realm of science and to find vocational fulfillment among his beloved tools and greasy gadgets. The lawyer said goodbye to a dream of his own, but he had said hello to the dream of his son; and in the renunciation of his own private wishes, that father gave the greatest blessing and the finest bequest to his child who was permitted to live his own life rather than become the elongated shadow of his father's ambition.

Unconditional love, unconditional acceptance, unconditional respect—these are three basic laws for the honoring of sons and daughters. There is a fourth important law: Give your child truth as well as respect; prepare him for the world as it is—a complex reality of good, bad and indifferent. Teach him quietly and simply in childhood and more completely in adolescence that the universe in which we live is filled not only with risks and dangers, but also with ruthless and selfish men and women. In our own way and at the appropriate moment, we should tell our children what Marcus Aurelius used to say to himself each morning, "Prepare, my soul, to meet today the liar, the cheat, the thief." While at first this may seem a counsel of cynicism and education for despair, it is in fact quite the opposite. It is part of the realistic education of our sons and our daughters. We should tell them that they should be prepared likewise to meet the wise, the good, the noble, the saintly; but we should not give them a false impression of what the universe is like and what life is like, and of what human nature is like, lest some day, in adolescence or in maturity, they batter their heads bloodily against the stone wall of reality which they have not been adequately trained to recognize. I do not believe that we should delude our children with fairy stories and fantasies, with illusions of all-goodness, all-beauty, all-purity that would make it impossible for them ever to make a genuine adjustment to the inevitable compromises

178

that life demands of them. The mother who keeps her daughter wrapped in cotton and shielded with the silken spools of illusion and the father who shields his son from the knowledge of the evil in the world—these parents are sowing a harvest of sadness, of disillusionment and later pessimism for their children and their children's children. "Know the worst about life, and work and hope for the best about life"—this is a motto that should be etched in the consciousness of fathers and mothers as they deal with their offspring. Of course this education for reality, this preparation for truth, should not be presented harshly, intemperately, unwisely. Children should absorb from their fathers and mothers realistic and unperturbed clarity about the universe—a sense of the world's disappointments as well as its blessings. Much later heartache can be avoided by the son and the daughter thus exposed to the truth, whether it is unconsciously absorbed from parental attitudes rather than from parental creeds. Such spirits will be able to take their places realistically, courageously and undefeatedly among the builders of a truer, nobler, juster, more compassionate order of life.

Finally, give your child a deep faith. Do not, because of your own mental indolence or indifference rob your son or your daughter of that great blessing of a religious philosophy of life which will take into consideration all the disillusionment and dark shadows of the universe and nevertheless find life worth living and God worth serving. Children readily respond to a negative or an affirmative approach to the universe from the parental environment, and I say that is why a creative and rich and joyous religion is so vital. You will honor your son and your daughter not when you allow his soul to remain void of any true belief in man or in God, but when you enable him to imitate you and to fill his reservoir from your overflowing spring of faith. If yours is empty, how can your child hope to quench the parched throat of his soul?

These, then, are some of the basic laws for honoring your son and your daughter. Give your children unconditional love, a love that is not dependent on report cards, clean hands, popularity, or winning a place in the dramatic society or on the high school football team. Do not allow your boy or girl ever to gain the impression that your love for him is contingent upon prizes or beauty or a success. In the second place, give your children a sense of your whole-hearted acceptance, acceptance of their human frailties as well as their abilities and virtues. Show them by your acts and by your words that you *like* them as well as *love* them, that you respect their interests and creative outlets, even though these may differ widely from your own particular pattern. Above all, give your children your permission to grow up to make their own lives independent of you, and independent also of your particular desires and ambitions. Give them a sense of truth; make them aware of themselves as citizens of a dangerous universe, a universe in which there are many obstacles as well as fulfillments, and prepare them for human nature in all its varieties and forms and variabilities. Show them that they must anticipate meeting in their lifetimes pitfalls and snares, and fickleness on the part of human beings from whom they expect faithfulness. Do not make the mistake of giving your children a picture of the world that is painted in unrealistic colors in which there are lights but no shadows. Give your children a sense of proportion in the landscape of the world, a sense of the reality of life with its lights and its shadows, of human nature with its goodness and its evils, and then bestow upon your child the blessings of your faith, a faith that is rooted in the trustworthiness of God and the trustworthiness of life itself. Unconditional love, unconditional acceptance, unconditional respect, unconditional truth and faith—these are the laws of honoring your son and your daughter. Out of these laws will be built the Declaration of Independence for the coming generation, a spiritual and psychic and emotional independence that, in turn, will make the world free, democratic, safe, creative.

Of course I do not deny that parents have rights just as children have. As parents we should not demand the impossible of ourselves. If in our home there is a firm, absolutely unchanging flow of love and acceptance and respect, our children can stand occasional earthquakes and lightning flashes of anger. They should not expect perfection of us any more than we should demand perfection of them. It is not so much a matter of doing this or that, of acting in this particular way or that particular way on one day or another. It is the total picture, the whole context that is important. The home should be a sanctuary in which there is balance, the achievement of the golden mean between extremes of total dependence and total indpendence, between absolute freedom, and absolute authoritarianism, which gives no leeway to the aspirations, the goals, the dreams of the coming generation—a well-run democracy where the rights of all, young and old, are respected and the duties of all are fulfilled. When the noble commandment of religion "Honor thy father and thy mother" is supplemented by the new insight "Honor thy son and thy daughter," we shall begin the journey that will lead at last to individual serenity, family unity and social peace.

CHAPTER EIGHT

The Art of Living

CHILDHOOD:
HOW CAN WE MAKE IT HAPPY?

Man is a portrait painter all his life; he is an artist daubing the canvas of existence with the many colored brushes of his feelings, his thoughts, his aspirations. Sometimes the portraits that we paint reveal a maturing sense of form and balance, a keen awareness of the proper relationship between light and shadow. Other life portraits have a sprawling, incoherent quality to them—like the crayon drawings of little children. The true art of living consists in moving successfully from the relatively formless portraiture of childhood through the often angry, violent canvases of adolescence into the proportioned balance and beauty of maturity, giving way at last to the twilight brush strokes of age.

In a sense, every human life is a one-man show and every day of our lives finds us adding a line to or subtracting a color from the canvases of our careers; in another sense, life is an art gallery where many canvases are displayed, and as we walk from one to the other, we are exalted and instructed by the rich variety of composition, by the charm or the terror of the landscape recorded on the retina of our souls.

Each of us has just one canvas at his disposal, his life; it is a canvas with many layers like some ancient masterpiece that has been painted over several times. We are all acquainted with striking stories of the discovery of an "old master" which is revealed under the searching chemicals of an "art-detective." The analogy to human life is striking. We paint first our awkward lines and grotesque figures of childhood, and then we cover that first portrait, with all its honest revelation of our fears and loves, with a new surface, first of adolescence and then of maturity. Peel off the scene that covers the canvas today, however, and beneath it you will find the hidden landscape of youth; peel off that paint and you will encounter the child's vision.

The truth is that today many men and women make out of their life portraits strange and horrifying surrealist scenes. I look at the art gallery of the twentieth century and I see many mysterious murals painted by frustration and fear. What characterizes the lives of myriads of men and women is what is found in some of the works of Dali—a piece of bone here, a broken clock, a broken chair on which stands a violin without strings. At first glance, the paintings of the cubists, the surrealists, the abstractionists, have a mad quality about them; then one senses they are not so mad after all, for they reflect the "broken-off" quality in so much of real life.

The art of living in this complex age is not achieved by simple good will alone. If we wish to know how to paint a harmonious rather than a grotesque canvas, we have to take lessons, to know something about the chemistry of the various dyes and colors, to become instructed in line and texture, light and shadow, to become acquainted with the history of art, studying the examples of failures as well as of masterpieces, and then and then only are we ready to put brush to canvas. All of these requirements are found in the realm of living itself. We need science as well as good will and love to make a success out of our existence and the existence of our children. As we look at the world today and stand aghast at its follies and tragedies, we must realize that what is wrong with our age has been made wrong by children—children who grow up physically but not morally, emotionally, spiritually. When I speak, therefore, of "childhood: how can we make it happy?" I am speaking not merely of personal joy in the family circle, but likewise of saving a world from misery and destruction. Unhappy children are the vandals who burned down the house of peace and stoned the windows of justice. A child is rejected by a mother; he waits thirty years ofttimes until he can in his turn reject and wreck goodness, creativeness, hope. More militarists than we suspect take vengeance against their own childhood by killing and causing to be killed in the name of patriotism. They are doing what they yearned to do in the days when they were frustrated, rejected or beaten. Much of the misery of life is caused by the postponed revenge for childish hates and fears.

History may or may not be interesting to a layman; but the personal history of the individual man or woman is indispensable for understanding social movements, both good and evil. The time bomb of childhood is ticking away in every human heart; it may explode and ruin only the dwelling place of the individual, or it may be powerful enough to strew wreckage over a whole neighborhood; with tyrants and dictators, the time bomb of private frustration and hate may blow up continents. It is only with true maturity and with genuine insight that we come to remove the detonating pin from the buried bomb of our early years, and through that removal become builders rather than destroyers of the life around us.

The gruesome examples of what unhappy childhood can do are all around us: in our divorce courts, our mental hospitals, and in homes of quiet desperation punctuated from time to time with the revelry of willed forgetfulness. Nor are these the only examples. Competitiveness, ruthlessness, lovelessness, the worship of wrong standards, the volcano of inner fears boiling beneath the hard outer crust of competence or arrogance, the way a man outsmarts his neighbor, punishes his child, dominates his wife, or the way a woman becomes a sieve through which all the grain of affection passes unnoticed, or a sponge absorbing and taking in but seldom giving—such men and women are themselves elongated shadows of their own childhood when they were warped or twisted by the adult world, when they were influenced by the example of father or mother to take but not to give, to hit or to be hurt, to master or to be mastered, to cling or to stand alone. One thing is certain—that the real shadow that every human being carries with him as long as he lives is that of his childhood. Modern science teaches us what those shadows look like. One is a hunchback, bent over with the burden of parental expectation; another is a timid shadow quietly weeping in the closet of self-pity; a third is the shadow of a child locked out of the room of maternal love because a new guest has come, a new arrival in the nursery of the family. Many are the shadows that everyone carries with him. The art of living is to learn how to fill out shadows and to deal with them. Straighten up, hunchback, carry your own expectations; come out of the corner, ghost of self-pity, you are strong now and others accept you where you were once rejected; put away your knife, specter of hate, shadow of anger; cease trembling, little shadow of anxiety, you are stronger now than your parents were, taller and straighter—no more bowing of your knees, little shadow, to the demanding king or the imperious queen of your nursery.

185

I have tried to express poetically what the science of human personality analyzes in prose, namely, that life becomes ruined or rich as a result of childhood experiences. The fortunate thing, of course, is that man is a revisable document and that the errors of the first edition can be corrected and even eliminated through later proofreadings in adolescence or in adulthood. The basic text, however, is there from our first few years upon earth, and it is quite possible to make the printer—human life—re-edit the manuscript. Excessive competitiveness, anxiety, hostility, suspiciousness, all originate in the nursery years. That is why, if we want a world of peace and not violence, love and not hate, cooperation and not murder, justice and not selfishness, we have to learn how to make childhood more happy. No nobler task could be pursued by our generation.

It is awfully difficult to see ourselves and our shortcomings. That is why an indirect approach, at first seemingly remote from our own existence, can give us needed insight and perspective. We find such an indirect approach to childhood, its happiness and unhappiness, in such diverse realms as anthropology and biography. In New Guinea, the Manus live as merchants. The Manus are as aggressive and as hard in their competitive life as any business dealer in our own commercial world. Each member of the tribe must be shrewd and remorseless, must allow no one to get the better of him. Marriage among the Manus is a very cold calculation; love means very little; children are reared without affection. The boys and girls grow up hard and anxious.

Among the primitive people of Alor in the Lesser Sunda Islands, the discipline of the children is very inconsistent and the children become disorganized personalities because they have no sure or secure source of love.

Among the mountain Arapesh of New Guinea we find a su-

186

perb illustration of the way to give children happiness rather than hardness and insecurity. The ideal of this culture is kindliness. Everyone shares his food. When a big job is to be done, the whole village takes part. Every child growing up is coddled and loved. The Arapesh give a warm welcome and deep affection to children; every child is treated as valuable. As a result, in this tribe there is little hostility or insecurity or ruthless competition. The Arapesh do not kill themselves or others for either power or prestige.

From the realm of biography we can find unforgettable examples of children ruined as far as happiness is concerned not merely because of society, but because of their family structure. Lord Byron, for example, had a scoundrel for a father and a flighty, impulsive woman for a mother. He never knew to whom he belonged or where he belonged. He yearned all his life for simple acceptance. As Professor Gardner Murphy describes it, "Byron wanted a regard for himself as a person. . . . His fundamental sickness was lack of self-love and self-acceptance." He had been rejected early in life and his own inner response to himself was rejection and self-scorn. The shadow of his childhood darkened all his poetry and all his life.

And an even more striking example is found in the life story of Franz Kafka, the great Czech Jewish novelist. His novels and short stories reflect a tortured and lonely soul, as I pointed out in some detail in Chapter I. Here I wish to use his life story to illustrate the effects of a distorted childhood. He never could find himself. He believed that man also was lost in a chartless wasteland. His friend and biographer, Max Brod, points out that Kafka was a child-sacrifice to a tyrannical father. Franz was raised in the home of a tall, strong, domineering Jewish merchant, a self-satisfied member of the Jewish bourgeoisie. He had made his own way in the world and he looked with contempt upon the rather weak poetic boy, Franz. In a long letter to his father, Kafka described their relationship as a painfully sad one. Elsewhere, recalling a punishment received in childhood, he quoted from an essay of Swift, "Children should be brought up only away from their families, not by their parents." "I was a nervous child," Kafka went on to say. "I can't believe that a friendly word, taking me by the hand, a friendly glance, would not have got me to do anything that was wanted . . . but I was a mere nothing to my father."

There is an unforgettable description of how Franz was taken by his father several times a year to the orthodox synagogue in Prague; and there how the young novelist saw how little meaning the Hebrew prayers had for his father. It was only in later life that Franz learned Hebrew and came to love Judaism through his own studies. In his boyhood, as he put it, his father tried to give him Judaism, but "your Judaism trickled away drop by drop as you tried to hand it on."

Brod brilliantly indicates that the novelist Kafka was like the great German poet, Heinrich von Kleist; neither ever got over his first childhood impressions. Kleist wanted his Prussian military family to admire and trust him, a poet, but he never obtained that admiration or that trust. "Parents are really the first problems that a child comes up against. A man begins to duel with life and the world. First round, his parents . . . then life sends other opponents against him, schoolfellows, teachers, fellow citizens." Actually, many of us carry with us as long as we live the saber scars of those first duels, and some of us fall to the ground, wounded in our egos for life by the swordsmen, father and mother. More people than we know suffer from those wounds, have a kind of subtle hemophilia—a blood system that flows too freely after the first wounds have appeared to heal.

Kafka, the novelist of human aloneness, once paid a tribute to another author in these memorable words: "He sits in himself as a first-class oarsman sits in his own boat and could sit in any boat." There are pathos and poignancy in that picture of a man secure within himself. Kafka was never secure because his father had always made him feel weak, worthless, valueless. In one of his writings, Kafka has a character ask "And your address?" to which the answer is "No fixed abode."

That is the story of unhappy children and unhappy adults: "No fixed abode."

In order to obtain a fixed abode, a secure dwelling place in the midst of life, in order to make childhood happy, what must we do? We must understand in the first place what children require, what they can take from the adult world and what they cannot take, and finally what they must be given, spiritually as well as psychologically, if their first painting upon the canvas of life is to have any beauty or order or promise.

Who is the child? He is a bit of protoplasm which in the human species has a long period of dependence upon father, mother and the adult world. In the first year of his life, he is still building sensitive walls of security about the tender acreage of his mind and nervous system. He cannot stand much rage or frustration in this first year. He begins to toddle, to walk, then to talk, and so to pass through the varying stages of his life growth. He is at first a monarch in the family love and he then is sent into exile—at least he feels it as exile. When another monarch comes (a baby brother or sister), he begins to become angry, to control this anger as he is punished for it, to find new outlets in school for his muscles and his growing mind and for the sturdy little core of independence that enables him to stand upon his feet, separated from the protecting arms of father and mother.

What does this child require—in addition to physical sustenance? He requires, in the first place, an unlimited diet of love, a sense of security in the midst of his dependence, a tolerance for his weakness and inevitable shortcomings, forbearance in the presence of his angers and hostilities and in general the principle of hope. "In spite of your little angers and tantrums, your fantasies and your failure," one must say to him, to let him know, "I, your parent, love you, beneath it all, through it all."

Many of the problems of later life arise from the fact that the human infant is dependent longer than any other creature on earth. The duration of this period can indeed be a blessing; it enables the child to experiment in safety, always knowing that there are the protecting arms of the adult world around. In this period of dependency, the child's mind is plastic, curious, growing, at least in part free from the anxiety the beasts of the field experience about food and shelter—cripplingly early. There is, however, another side to the coin of dependency: the temptation of the child to remain reliant and parasitic upon the mother or father for too long a time, and the equal temptation of the parent to prolong that dependency until it becomes a lifelong habit, a fear of freedom and anxiety about growth.

No, life has not arranged an easy destiny for parents or for children. The goal of existence should be for us to move from babyhood, where we are parasites, to adulthood, where we become patrons of life. How often, however, do we go astray! The first true condition for happiness in childhood is for the parent to give the child a gradually increasing independence while still giving him love. In the second place, the father and mother must be prepared for aggression and temper tantrums and for the gradual transformation of these hostile impulses from personal hate to an impersonal combativeness where the normal aggressive energies are harmlessly drained off in sports and games.

The art of living never consists in denying or killing our human endowments, but in channeling them properly and converting them wisely.

Now, there are things a child can stand. He can stand punishment if it is meted out with fairness and with consistency. The best kind of punishment is the withdrawal of certain privileges temporarily. The child of six or ten should understand quite well that "Mother and Father love you in spite of this misdeed or error. It is just this particular act that they do not like; they embrace and accept you even while rejecting this minor trait or particular act." A child can accept fair and equitable punishment; in fact, if he does not receive it, his conscience, which he has taken over from the models of father, mother, older brother or sister, will begin to torment him. A child can accept authority but not rejection.

Human life is complicated because there is polarity in all our natures. We love and we hate, we embrace and we reject; and we start life with this dual approach of taking in and expelling. Life is complicated also because we find it hard to achieve the golden mean between extremes. Parents ofttimes torture themselves because of guilt feelings or anger feelings toward their offspring.

Part of the wisdom needed in our day lies just here. Parents should become more relaxed toward themselves and toward their children. Creative relaxation is needed in the family environment. Suppose a four-year-old, angry at the arrival of a new baby, becomes impossible, unmanageable almost. The father or the mother should recognize that a harsh reaction on their part is normal, understandable, inevitable, yet many torment themselves because they do not conform to an ideal picture of parenthood or because they feel that they have failed. The great contribution of Judaism about time—the recognition that there is a flow in the world from the past through the present into the future—should be a benediction. The mood of anger, the spasm of fear, the feeling of passion—these will pass away, the dark cloud vanish. We make too much of an idol out of permanency and needlessly afflict ourselves with the thought that a trait in our child or a mood in ourself is here to stay. Judaism, which emphasized not the static but the dynamic, which did not stress Being as the Greeks did but rather Becoming, can give us sanity in this art of living with childhood. It is not what the boy or girl is in detail at a particular moment in the time-flow of his growth but the general direction of growth, the majority of the moods and attitudes which can be shaped and changed without pampering. Such sanity born out of a religion like Judaism, can make both childhood and parenthood happier.

There are some things that a child cannot stand without life-long ill effects. He cannot stand utter inconsistency from the grown-up world. He cannot accept disapproval and total rejection. He needs applause as he needs milk; he needs to feel himself valuable in the circle of the family.

He cannot take in his early years the frustration given by a stern and demanding parent who wants to have his offspring achieve independence too soon. Many an adult is looking all his life for the lost Atlantis of love and warm dependence. There is such a thing as being underspoiled and there certainly is such a thing as being overspoiled.

Many parents in today's world overindulge their children. They give them everything material, encourage them to outdo the neighboring child not only in marks and in popularity, but in clothes and possessions and vanity. Why do parents make such mistakes? Partly perhaps because of their own guilt feelings.

They want to shower everything upon their children to compensate for their own early poverty, or because at times they feel their children a burden, or are hostile to them. Whatever the reason, overindulgence is a tragic crime against the next generation. A child denied little, made the center of both gifts and admiration, is not prepared for the real hardships of life. Such a child will grow into an adult who demands to be admired, indulged, taken care of. He will not be able to make the compromises or the postponements necessary for maturity. The golden-haired child becomes bald under the heavy winds and thick snows of reality. Such men and women, unprepared for life, ruin their marriages, constantly look for leaders and are ripe for the plucking of dictatorship with its promises of security.

The opposite attitude makes for unhappiness in childhood: the giving of inadequate understanding, love and protection. Children so treated often grow up to be cynics, skeptics, criminals or misanthropes.

Another great source of unhappiness in childhood, as we have already noted in Chapter VII, is the parents' desire to have their children fulfill the parents' own aspirations. Fathers and mothers who demand what Sophocles described in *Antigone* as "dutiful offspring"—parents who demand serviceable children, who will make up to them for what they have missed in life— also paint a terrible, ghastly portrait.

Children should be loved and respected as personalities in their own right, not as potential atonements for their parents' failures. Here, too, we must learn to become suspicious about ourselves. We begin life many times with a desire for omnipotence—for power over things and persons. Life defeats us, and we know that we are not either all-wise or all-powerful. How frequently is the home made the experimental laboratory where a man or woman, robbed of his dreams of omnipotence and omniscience in the outer world, tries to play the role of a little god, pulling puppets' strings in his family circle.

"Childhood—how can we make it happy?" We must know that our children require secure love, tolerant understanding of their strange traits and fleeting hostilities; they require from us conscience patterns—good models they can imitate for their own growth. Our children require from us patience without comparisons. Each child should be accepted on his own terms and allowed to grow according to his own inner rhythm without constantly being compared with other children and deprecated when he fails to measure up.

Our children can take discipline when it is given with fairness and equality, and we as parents do not need to feel as though we were ogres when we grow occasionally angry or restrictive or petulant. Let the children always sense the calm stream of our love supporting the bark of their existence, even though from time to time there are storms and squalls of disapproval and punishment. Let us avoid with our children the two great sources of unhappiness—overindulgence or frustration and the use of our offspring as the vehicle to reach our private goals.

In addition to all these psychological requirements for happiness in childhood, there is a spiritual requirement. Parents and children have to live in a shared world. That is why shared religious experience is so fundamental to healthy-mindedness and sanity. Kafka felt himself isolated from his father's Jewishness because the holidays and ideals of Judaism were never explained to the child, nor were they lived vitally and warmly.

I think of the mystery of Jewish survival throughout the ages, and I believe that part of that survival occurred because fathers and mothers gave to their children shared values—the importance of the study of the Torah, the communion of mind and of spirit at the Holy Days and at Succoth and Passover.

May we in our generation have the wisdom to paint a portrait of each new life, not perfect but growing in beauty. As we paint that portrait with love, security, inner tolerance and religious wisdom, we shall indeed create a universe, a little universe of fulfillment beyond frustration, of peace beyond violence.

ADOLESCENCE:
How Can We Solve Its Problems?

The scale of life today is vast indeed. We often feel: What are we? what is our life? In the midst of world events, we feel more frequently than ever before the insignificance of our own personal existences. We regard ourselves sometimes as grains of sand near the vast pyramids of economic and political struggle.

Occasionally we feel guilty about preoccupation with our own private concerns and personal worries, our family problems, our human joys. Yet we ought not to feel guilty about such preoccupation. The truth is that we men and women have neither the power nor the opportunity to solve directly the great social issues of our time. Our primary responsibility is for the lives that we lead and the other lives that we influence directly within the circle of our family and of our small community. Indirectly, of course, we touch the hem of the garment of the whole world, and our deeds and attitudes make for health or disease in the bloodstream of humanity. Our truest influence lies close at hand. We carry ourselves with us as long as we live and wherever we go. The ripple of the stone of decision which we cast into the lake of life is easy to discern close at home, but it grows fainter and fainter as it touches the distant shores of society at large. Yes, let us have no feelings of guilt about an attempt to achieve wisdom and clarity about the "art of living" for ourselves and for our children. If we obtain these objectives within the circle of the family, the family of mankind will be blessed with a new sanity and a new hope.

The problems of our world are found in the fact that we live in an adolescent culture. By adolescent culture I mean a culture that is excessively competitive and morally indecisive, a culture that vacillates from day to day between acceptance and rebellion. Such a culture is adolescent in the sense that the world does not know its own mind and has no sense of security about its values and its standards. The shadow of adolescence is everywhere in the twentieth century. We men and women who are chronologically adult find it difficult to solve the conflicts of adolescence because we ourselves are still psychically and emotionally involved in the battles of our youth which never came to any final settlement within us. A truce was declared in our life, but we never achieved a final peace treaty with the ambitions, conflicts, fears and hopes of our own adolescent period.

Life is so complicated, tragic and confused because there really are so few adults among us. Maturity is a rare jewel, beyond price in the market of men. Adolescence is not only a stage that we have lived through but a stage of life that lives on in us. We may have repressed it; we may have forgotten about its turmoil and its tumult; but let us have no illusions: we carry the scars of our youth with us, and its attitudes shape, color and mold the clay of our spirit as long as we live.

Now, to understand life, we must turn not only to the laws of psychological science but also to the eternal insights of religion. A religion like Judaism, for example, contains within it certain allegories and parables that are as deep as any of the myths of Plato, and also certain principles that are the guiding laws of conduct and of thought.

Recently I have been reading the monumental work of Professor H. A. Wolfson of Harvard on the great Jewish philosopher, Philo. The author of this important study points out how Philo, two thousand years ago, harmonized much of Greek philosophy with Biblical teaching—the wisdom of Athens with the revelations of Jerusalem. Now, just as Philo discerned in certain of the verses of the Old Testament—in its portrayal, for example, of angels and messengers of God—the embodiment of the incorporeal ideas of Plato, and found in some of the great stories of Genesis allegories quite parallel to the doctrines of Aristotle and the Stoics, so I think that we today can find in that eternal treasure house of wisdom, the Old Testament, psychological profundity, the parallel to many of the insights of Freud, the modern Plato and Aristotle in the realm of human nature.

You are all familiar with the immortal story of the liberation from Egypt. Moses led the Hebrews out of the land of bondage, as a parent leads his children. The Book of Exodus in Chapter 14 describes what happened as they marched together toward the Promised Land. The people grew afraid and they turned in bitterness upon Moses; and they said it would be better for them to serve the Egyptians than to die in the wilderness. In other words, they wanted to turn back, to halt the march of their progress toward mature freedom. They turned upon their father figure, their liberator, with words of hatred and acts of rebellion. They wanted to go back to the country from which they had escaped, to regress to the dwelling place of their past with all of its hardships and pain and hunger. They were terrified of the unknown which lay ahead of them.

Moses, mature leader that he was, understood the murmurings and the bitterness and the ingratitude of the people—his children. There were moments when he grew deeply discouraged, when the burden seemed too heavy for him to bear, when he wanted to surrender, when he cried out unto God to lift the burden of responsibility and care from his shoulders. These moments of weakness, however, were fleeting; the permanent attitude as well as conduct of Moses was that of a patient father taking the abuse of his fledglings, the revolt of his adolescents, and conveying to them the message of God: "Speak unto the children of Israel, that they go forward."

If in our own century a creative French writer like Sartre could take the ancient Greek story of Orestes as the subject matter for a provocative drama, *The Flies,* if the matchless modern novelist, Thomas Mann, could find in the story of Joseph and his brothers the symbol of man's eternal descent into the pit of tragedy in order to be purified and ascend toward the heights of creative giving, we can find in the story of Moses and the Hebrew slaves the most valuable psychological wisdom, not only an allegory in religion but guiding laws for human nature and human interrelatedness.

Has human nature ever been portrayed more vividly than in this portrait of the Hebrew serfs who wanted to be liberated and at the same time wanted to return to Egypt when they were faced with the unknown and the difficulties and hardships? They wanted to return to Egypt with all its known horrors of slavery rather than to go forward toward the unknown Promised Land! I think of this whole section of the Bible as a superb and poetic intuition about the nature of adolescence. The adolescent yearns to go forward to his promised land, but he also wishes at times to return, to regress to the land of childhood, to his private

Egypt with all its serfdom, its dependency. The parent who spurs the adolescent on to maturity is often treated and regarded as Moses was by the people he liberated—hated, reviled, murmured against. Now, as Moses lost patience at moments and groaned under the burden of an ungrateful people, so fathers and mothers are tempted to lose patience and groan under the burden of their inconsistent adolescent boys and girls.

That story in Exodus is as full of insight as anything in Plato or in Aeschylus. In Moses is portrayed the man of maturity; in the Hebrew slaves of Egypt the traits of adolescence are drawn with unerring accuracy. How can we deal with adolescence? In a preliminary way we can say that we must have something of the character of Moses: his patience, his perspective, his reliance upon process. Moses continued to lead the people with the patience which comes from the attitude of "nevertheless"; he had the perspective to recognize that, as the years passed, Israel would change and grow, and so he was able to stand the betrayal of his life's mission, the rejection of his work, when the people he had emancipated, to whom he had given everything, danced around the golden calf while he was trying to bring down to them the law of God. Moses had faith in Progress; it was not what the Jews were at that particular moment in their evolution, but what they would become in the time flow of the future, that made all his love and sacrifice worthwhile. Moses learned not to judge or condemn the adolescent slaves of Egypt but to love them and to lead them in spite of their backsliding and their revolt against his wisdom—to love them and to lead them in the conviction that they would yet come to the mountain of maturity.

The task of our generation—of moving from adolescence to maturity—is an inescapable challenge to be met if we are to

survive. Maturity is the prerequisite for any human future. No
if we are to achieve even the beginnings of emotional adulthoo
we shall have to understand the adolescent, who he is and wh
he needs, and above all, what he lived through in those stran
and contradictory years between childhood and manhood.

Professor Arnold Toynbee, in the opening chapter of
book *Civilization on Trial,* points out that the prophets of Isra
through their own experience anticipated Aeschylus' discove
that learning comes through suffering. This is the leitmotif
adolescence: that learning comes through suffering. We ou
selves in our more mature years may have forgotten or represse
some of that suffering, but the pain is undeniable—the pain
growing up, of being transformed from the loved, protecte
ofttimes overindulged child moving toward the arena of adu
experience, the world of harsh reality. Adolescence is a time
great suffering for those who are living through it as well as fc
the parents and the family. The pain is sometimes quiet, hidde
inarticulate; at other times it is quite overt and may manifes
itself in many grotesque and bizarre forms.

What takes place in adolescence? A boy who has live
through his early years as the center of a little universe, at leas
of his parents' universe, and who has then entered into the rela
tively placid period of later childhood—the "latency" period—
suddenly finds himself overtaken by a torrential storm, a verit
able tornado of new feelings, emotions, conflicts. The difference
between adolescence and childhood is the difference between a
tranquil brook and a raging ocean.

Let us try to understand, first of all, the basic conflict of the
adolescent, his essential fears, his dominant needs, his outstanding character traits and his overwhelming moods.

The basic conflict of the adolescent is between his desire to grow up and his yearning to remain a child. There is a civil war raging within the youth between his feelings of dependence and his aspirations for independence. With part of his nature he wants to be taken care of, to be loved, to be given security; and with another part of his nature he rejects these longings as infantile, unworthy of a grown person. Adolescents feel guilty about their yearnings for protection. Quite often they tear themselves to pieces in this unacknowledged battle between the childish and the mature elements in their makeup. Young boys and girls just entering adolescence are starting that civil war within their own souls, and upon the way their personal conflicts are settled depends the future serenity and creativity of each individual.

What is the great fear of the adolescent? It is the great fear of himself. We know now that the dread of the unknown is one of the most soul-shattering horrors that man has to face. Well, the youth faces the unknown within himself. Strange gusts of emotion sweep across the open prairie of his spirit. Tremendous changes are occurring within his very organism; his glands are shaking the house of his habits the way a great storm twists and uproots a young tree in a forest. At times the young man or woman feels as though he had been taken possession of by demons—the demons of anger, hostility, violence, sexuality. The adolescent is swept with fear of his powerful instinctual urges; he has not lived long enough to know whether he will be able to master them. He is like a traveler who has come suddenly to a new country without a Baedeker or map or a knowledge of the language spoken in this untraversed territory.

What are the essential needs of the adolescent? He has a need, in the first place, for status, for belonging. There is nothing that he longs for more than acceptance and approval by his contemporaries. He may be and often is quite secretive with father and

201

mother, convinced that they cannot understand his drives and hungers and yearnings; but he will do almost anything to be given the stamp of citizenship in the realm of his friends and comrades. This is a time of great conformity to the demands of "the gang." This is also the period when herd warmth is most essential.

It is important to understand that the appeal of mass movements like fascism and communism is directed not only to the childlike yearning for protection and security—the satisfaction of the dependence need of human nature—but also toward the adolescent needs of grown men and women. The mass movements of our age have known how to play upon the hunger for acceptance and belonging which is at the root of the adolescent uncertainty about status. It is just because the youth is profoundly perturbed about his place and position in the universe, and particularly in the universe of his fellow men, that authoritarian systems guaranteeing the paradise of belonging have such an enormous capacity to seduce and hypnotize the youthful mind.

There are other needs of the adolescent—for personal adequacy, for personal identity. The young men or the young girls in their teens are constantly striving to find an answer to the question "Who am I?" They are seeking a new address, as it were, on the street of life. In addition to this need for personal adequacy and identity, there is a need for a rather free experimentation with new roles and the achievement of new selves. Adolescence is a period of enormous fertility as far as fantasy goes. The youth dreams of himself as artist, poet, scientist, reformer, world redeemer. There is an enormous amount of idealism and of intellectualism in this period of human development. Part of it is genuine, and part of it can be understood thoroughly only as a reaction and a protection against the powerful biological drives which frighten and terrify the growing personality.

Many boys and girls in this stage of life throw themselves with enormous passion into intellectual achievements and into idealistic movements. Part of this is certainly a flight from the primitive emotions and passions which they do not understand but which they experience as a menace to their adjustment in the familial environment. Adolescent personalities may turn to music, art or science as havens of refuge from themselves and their urges; they may flee to reason with its pale-white security as a fortress against the besieging enemy of emotion and passion. What starts out in this stage of life as a refuge—intellectualism and idealism—may become in later experience a constructive and creative way of life. In the youthful period, however, the taking on of the role of thinker or reformer or revolutionary is part of the essential experimentalism of the life process.

What is the character structure of the adolescent? Many indeed are the traits of youth. I would mention but two or three in this context. Young people fluctuate and vacillate from day to day; they do not know what to believe, how to act. They are unstable in mood and in deed. In the second place, adolescence is characterized by a tremendous competitiveness. A human being at this stage of existence is so deeply uncertain about his worth, his value and his future that he constantly has to test himself and to prove himself. One has only to look at American society to see that this adolescence has not been outgrown; in fact it has been magnified in the marketplace of our society. Men and women are engaged in a ceaseless quest for power and more power, prestige and more prestige. People who are like the troubled sea, who never know any inner tranquillity because they are constantly trying to achieve more success, reveal their immaturity, their unripeness; they are still fixated on the adolescent level of development.

When I said earlier that ours is an adolescent culture, I had in mind primarily its ruthless competitiveness, which brings about not merely physical and nervous breakdowns in individuals but also a general breakdown of moral and ethical standards. Life should be more than a race, but for millions of men and women in America and throughout the world, life is just that and nothing more. It is a quest for power. The great philosopher Nietzsche understood how hungry man is for power; he is hungry for it, however, when he himself is insecure, frightened, uncertain. Our world is immature just because it makes a god out of power rather than out of goodness. A society will never become adult so long as it remains imprisoned within the circle of adolescent striving. It is natural for a youth to test his abilities and to find out his capacities in comparison with those of his contemporaries; it is tragic when grown men and women remain so eternally unsure of themselves that they have to struggle to acquire trophies of applause as proof of their worth and value.

The adolescent, therefore, must be understood as a creature suffering from many mood swings, full of indecision, riven with instability, harnessed to the chariot of competition and rivalry, chained often to the death car of the quest for power. All of this turmoil within him creates the basic mood of youth—aloneness.

He does feel alone. He has had to give up childhood; he has surrendered, not without great pain and much grief, the relatively secure dwelling place of his earliest years upon earth; like Jacob in the Bible, he wrestles with angels and demons within his own spirit, and he feels himself deserted often, rejected more often, misunderstood most often. He is convinced that he is unique in the burden that he carries and the suffering that he endures. He has not learned how universal these moods and conflicts are; he has not become skillful enough to build lines of communication to the world as a whole; he feels himself an alien.

It is no wonder that the adolescent should feel himself quite often an alien. He walks upon a strange new road; it is a tortuous road with many rocks and sharp-pointed obstacles for the feet of the wanderer. He feels himself journeying through a jungle, at the mercy of wild beasts; the jungle, however, is within himself and the wild beasts are in his own heart. He is frightened and makes many noises to keep up his own courage. He not only whistles in the dark, but shouts and yells and flails his arms about often quite wildly in order to ward off the menacing creatures that he sees along the road. It makes no difference that actually these are fantasies of his own making; they are real to the youth. They are real as anger, aggression, violence, love, and lust are real. The adolescent does not understand that he is really walking where everyone else has walked—a road well trodden by humanity throughout all of the ages. Mistakenly he regards himself as a pioneer in this uncharted wilderness. His inner senses have not matured enough for him to detect any footprints of humanity along the road that he is treading. That time will come—the time when he will recognize that he is part of the unending pilgrimage of the human species from childhood dependence to adult independence, with the winding, often painful road joining the two worlds together.

In the meantime, adolescence and its conflicts must be understood by fathers and the mothers, if there is to be any hope for a creative and peaceful future. Not that it is easy for parents to tolerate the sudden metamorphosis that has taken place in their beloved offspring. If the youth feels himself alone, parents too feel that they have a stranger within the gates of their hearts. Something terrible has happened in the transition from childhood to adolescence. It is no wonder that many mothers and fathers experience a real fear of the stranger that now dwells within their house. What a difficult time this is for the whole family! The adolescent is bombarded within himself by all kinds of rockets and shells of emotion, anxiety, aspiration. He, in turn, bombards those who are nearest and closest to him. Parents have to come to recognize that they play the role of scapegoats. They are the safest scapegoats available to the next generation. The young person senses that there is a deep core of love in the hearts of his father and mother and that this core will not be destroyed by his bombardment. Therefore, he turns upon his parents as outlets for his own new emotions.

Parents have to understand that they are targets—convenient targets and also safe targets—for the aggressions and frustrations of their children. The adolescent often does not understand what he is doing; he is miserable because he is the victim of this tremendous conflict between his childish desires and his adult wishes, because many of his needs are not being satisfied as quickly as he wishes. He is miserable—and misery loves company. That is why so many adolescents try to bring their parents down to their level and why it is so important that mothers and fathers should not allow their own adolescent stage to be reborn. Nothing is more tragic than for parents to engage with youth in a kind of competitive struggle on the immature level of teen-age reaction patterns.

Fathers and mothers have to understand that in adolescence appearance is not reality. The great problem of philosophy throughout the ages—namely, how to distinguish between substance and illusion, between appearance and reality—is a problem that occurs most vividly on the adolescent level in our human journey. Often we mistake the symptoms for the causes and try to solve the essential difficulties of adolescence by attacking a minor phenomenon here or there. The truth is that adolescent boys and girls are constantly going through periods of testing their fathers and mothers to see whether they still love them, to see whether they still can take all the burdens, inconsistencies, and unpredictabilities that the adolescent places upon parental shoulders. Youth is often tortured and tormented by guilt feelings; it is aware of the surging tides of sex which it does not yet know how to manage; it is afraid of involvement and of closeness with father and mother. That is why there is often so much secretiveness among adolescents and why there is this strange pattern of identification with contemporaries and remoteness from the father and mother who have given so much in love and care throughout the years.

Only saints could take the rudeness and moodiness of adolescents with absolute equanimity. Fathers and mothers should not demand that kind of saintliness in themselves. It is hard to live with a changeling, a chameleon. Sometimes I wonder whether the essential problem of religion about justice in the world—that problem entitled theodicy: why do the righteous suffer and the wicked prosper—does not arise from this relationship between parents and children, parents and adolescents. Why is it there is so much complexity, so much suffering, so much pain, in the process of human growth? Perhaps the only satisfying answer is that given by the ancient sages: that we learn through our pain, we grow through our suffering.

Parents are wise when they understand the inevitability of that suffering and when they begin to prepare themselves for their hard lot during that particular stage of evolution which is called adolescence. They must be prepared to be placed under the microscope of criticism, to be deflated and devalued, to have their opinions rarely accepted and often denied. All of this is part of the process by which the young boy or girl is achieving emancipation, beginning to walk on the road to freedom and maturity. Much of the seeming enmity on the part of youth toward their parents is pure illusion; it just does not mean what it appears to mean; it is a step in the direction of liberation. Young people have to deflate their parents in order to feel their own inner worth and value; they engage in this scapegoat technique in order to make themselves independent.

How can parents be of help in the conflicts of adolescence? In the first place, I think that fathers and mothers must strive to achieve the golden mean that was basic to the ethics of Aristotle and appears as central in the philosophy of Maimonides. We today can adopt that principle in the relationship between parents and adolescent boys and girls. What it means is that there should be neither too great dependence nor too great independence given at that stage of life. Sometimes fathers and mothers have the unfortunate idea that children who out of fear or yearning for love remain completely dependent upon them, unrebellious, completely acquiescent, will have a happy future life in this world. I believe that is a tragic mistake. If young people do not go through certain phases of rebellion and revolt, do not test their own powers adequately, they will remain immature or neurotic all their lives. At the other extreme are to be found fathers and mothers who confer too great independence upon their adolescent offspring too early. The golden mean between extremes is the path of wisdom.

The second great art that parents must achieve if there is to be any harmony in life for their adolescent boys and girls is the art of proper detachment, proper distance and proper devotion. Fathers and mothers need detachment from the lives of their offspring. They should not expect to live their children's lives for them. What many religions have taught about the necessity for detachment, for a kind of wise perspective, is certainly necessary in the parent-adolescent relationship. Proper distance is also requisite, both psychic distance and physical distance. Separation as well as closeness can prove a blessing in this stage of human development. Finally, fathers and mothers must have a devotion to their adolescent boys and girls *in spite of* all the inconsistency, inconsiderateness, unpredictability of the youthful generation.

Here is one of the great truths that we have to acquire. It does not take any profound wisdom on the part of mothers and fathers to love an infant. Here is the newborn child, weak, helpless, utterly dependent upon the strength of the father and mother. In those early months of life, in the first several years of life, the easiest and most natural thing in the world is for fathers and mothers to coo over the baby and to find great compensation in the warm response of love from the infant. It does not take a philosopher to love the infant with all its cuteness and softness and warmth and lovableness. In the early stage of the parent-child relationship, love is love because of, not in spite of. It is in adolescence that we have to achieve as parents the greater art and the deeper philosophy of maintaining an unchanged devotion in spite of the hardness and the harshness and the strangeness of our offspring.

Fathers and mothers of little babies live according to the pleasure principle: it is easy for them to give love; fathers and mothers of adolescent boys and girls have to live in accordance with the reality principle: it is difficult to show devotion, understanding, tolerance and forgiveness for all the peculiar and chameleonlike changes in mood and attitude from day to day and month to month. The triumph of the parent is achieved mainly at this testing period of mature devotion.

We have to have faith that the adolescent will be able to

achieve mastery and self-control. Growth is always painful, not only physically but emotionally and spiritually. "Learning through suffering" is the motto of youth and of age. The consolation that we can have is that multitudes of human beings have learned how to control their impulses and master their passions, and to move without too much tragedy from the unripeness of youth to the relative maturity of adulthood.

The greatest consolation can come to us when we understand the wisdom of such a religion as Judaism. The faith of Israel has always emphasized Becoming. Ours is a dynamic, not a static, world, taught the rabbis of old. It is this dynamism which is the source of hope in the relationship between parents and adolescents. If fathers and mothers consider the fleeting moods and the temporary attitudes of their offspring as permanent, then they will be miserable, and unhappy and tormented, and the climate of opinion in the household will be dark and ominous. I think that we can learn for our day a great lesson from the very philosophy of Judaism, which always believes that time is the great healer and the great gift of God to man. In the time flow of human development there are no fixed and final stages. There are processes going on. Life is a matter of direction, change, and growth—the triumph of process over fixity.

Let us take a page out of the teaching of Judaism as well as modern psychology and recognize that adolescence is not a fixed stage. It is merely one part of the road that we must traverse in our journey toward genuine maturity. Let us as parents come to understand, as Moses did with his adolescent Hebrew slaves from Egypt, that those for whom we do most will often be ungrateful, aggressive, secretive, strange, unappreciative, and that we will be the targets of their hostility. Let us do what Moses did thousands of years ago—continue to lead and to love our adolescents, confident that they will move with our help and strength from self-centeredness to self-fulfillment and human fulfillment. They walk during the years of their youth along a wasteland, a great desert, often without finding any oasis of understanding unless we provide that oasis. We can provide the shelter of our love if we will understand what is going on in the inner psyches of our children as they mature; and if we refuse to take the lawlessness and the unpredictability of adolescence as a permanent situation, they will yet move out of the dusty wasteland into the green valley of achievement and creation.

As fathers and mothers in our century gain these insights and this wisdom, there is a hope that the adolescent culture marred by so much brutal competitiveness will give way to a mature culture based upon genuine brotherhood and profound and joyous cooperation. Let us never forget the words of the great historian, Arnold Toynbee, "Life is not a harbor, it is a voyage."

MATURITY:
How Can We *Really* Attain It?

Our age is filled with nihilism. Many who have lost faith are filled with a kind of destructive rage against what they call the "delusion of belief" in anyone else. The nineteenth century saw the decline of faith in God, the twentieth century a catastrophic decline of faith in man. The disenchantment among tired liberals, as well as tired radicals and tired conservatives, is like a thick fog concealing any road and any destination. There was a time when the world seemed to be young in hope, when new social experiments were rooted in Utopian visions. Now it appears that both the experiments and the Utopias have collapsed

211

together and countless sensitive men and women feel that they have no home, spiritually or ideologically. The human race has become the wandering Jew; mankind feels itself in exile. This feeling generates an enormous amount of bitterness and a great deal of skepticism. If you cannot believe in anything, you are not too happy if your neighbor believes in something; you are tempted to explode his balloon of hope with the sharp knife of your disillusionment.

Pacifism, communism, socialism, capitalism, all of which have seemed at one time or another to be the final answer, to offer the ultimate Utopia, have in turn revealed glaring weaknesses and brutal shortcomings. Many of us today are like children, disconsolately weeping over fairy stories that have not proved true, crying our hearts out because our pet Utopias have receded into the infinite distance. Perhaps what is needed today is something of that ancient Jewish wisdom which forbade speculation about the coming of the Messianic Age, the time of arrival of Utopia— something of the Jewish wisdom which did not search for absolutes and did not grow unhappy in the attainment of merely partial answers. The nihilism of our time—that sophisticated cynicism which turns the dagger in all generous hopes and idealistic programs—is really a mark of immaturity. The mind of an adolescent does not find it easy to allow a brother or a sister to possess something denied himself. Many a philosopher or poet, bloodily and brutally exposing the presumed fallacies in man's faith in God, in man and in society, is still that adolescent restlessly bringing the world down to his own level of misery. To believe in partial answers, to work for limited goals, to sacrifice for finite objectives, to give to life without demanding any immediate pay envelope from the universe—these are some of the saving signs of maturity.

Shakespeare wrote, "Ripeness is all." If we equate ripeness with maturity, we can say that ours is certainly an unripe culture. There is so much of the child and adolescent in our make-up. Perhaps the first way to attain maturity is to learn how to transcend our useless, infantile and youthful attitudes. Those attitudes once were very normal and useful. A child quite understandably feels dependent and yearns for security; he would be rather strange, indeed abnormal, if in infancy or babyhood he rejected care, protection and love, in the interests of a self-asserted independence. Likewise, an adolescent who refuses to compete, to test his abilities, to race with his contemporaries, experiences a dangerous placidity that augurs ill for future happiness. There does come a time, however, when childish dependence and adolescent rivalry should be out of place—namely, in creative adulthood. We ought to outgrow our earlier phases of development the way we physically outgrow the clothes of childhood and youth.

Now, growing up to maturity is a painful process. That is why so many people seem to avoid it. When we come into a new area of experience, we feel like aliens and strangers and we mourn for the lost paradise of our earlier status.

I have recently come to think that adolescence at times is a grief situation, when we mourn the death of our childhood importance. We human beings do not merely have the capacity to bemoan the death of loved ones; we also have the capacity to mourn over our own lost selves and our lost roles. Are not the sullenness and morbidity of the adolescent sometimes to be interpreted as unconscious grief for the death of the child he once was, so precious, so secure, so exalted?

The truth that grief reactions occur not only at times of physical death but at other decisive moments in the evolution of a human life should make clear some confusing moods and behavior of human beings. The skittishness of the middle-aged Lothario who tries to act like a young blade of twenty, the feverish pursuit of power, success or pleasure, conceal beneath the surface mourning for a youth buried but now disinterred. The adolescent mourns for his lost childhood, the middle-aged man for his lost youth, and the aged for his waning power. The fear of death, of which the existentialists, primarily Martin Heidegger, speak so morbidly, arises not merely because our imagination can visualize and grieve over our future end, our inevitable corpse, but also because our minds actually grieve over our vanished past.

Those who remain chained to one particular level of growth are excessive mourners around the coffin of a beloved stage of life from which they cannot bear to be parted. That is why so many men and women remain children emotionally or stand still at the landing of adolescence, never quite daring to make the ascent to the broad but dizzying heights of maturity.

Now, when is a person relatively mature? By definition, he is adult when he ceases to indulge in the characteristic demands and reactions of the child or the adolescent. The child is primarily a "taking" creature, absorbing food, drinking in love, digesting information. Childhood is the stage of intake from life; adolesence continues this taking, demanding, self-centered approach; maturity is a supreme revolution, when the arrow of life moves outward instead of inward, when the personality is anxious to give, to share, to bestow, to become a parent of life. This is the pendulum swing of human destiny between taking and giving, swallowing and serving.

Authorities in psychology measure maturity by the degree to which a person manifests an "object-interest." A human being who is genuinely solicitous about the welfare of another person or truly sacrificial in the service of a great cause is mature. This is one of the most vital truths man has to learn. Religion long ago understood the necessity of an object-interest: "Thou shalt love thy neighbor as thyself. . . . What is hateful unto thyself do not do unto thy neighbor. . . . If I am for myself alone, what am I?"

Gifted theologians like Reinhold Niebuhr acquaint us with the dangers of egotism, more especially its subtle and disguised forms. So much of life is tainted, we are told, with self. Even when we give the appearance of being interested in a cause or movement outside ourselves, like nationalism or socialism or communism, the suspicion has grown that the larger object of our devotion is often only a blown-up version of ourselves: *My* nation is myself magnified a millionfold; *my* class is also myself endowed with the strength of a giant. True indeed is the accusation that much altruism is concealed self-interest.

Now, self-interest is in a sense inescapable. We begin our lives always as potential selves, and for the first few years we are not strong enough to give any surplus to the world. Our childhood is the stage when we deposit the coins of strength, health, and growing intelligence in the bank of experience. We are not ready to make loans because we do not have enough capital accumulated. It is only later in life, in genuine maturity, that we have sufficient credit stored up to enable us truly to give to others—to become benefactors, patrons and parents.

I have said that one great test of maturity is the ability to have a genuine interest in something beside one's self—a mate or a child or a friend or an ideal. To achieve such maturity is admittedly difficult because all the circumstances of life for so many years condition us toward immaturity. When I was a child, I was absorbing, taking in, dependent as no other species of earth is dependent for long years of shelter and protection. I came into adolescence, and once again I was forced into preoccupation with myself, with all of the strange explosions of glands and fears, rivalries and testing going on within my mind, making me often withdrawn and isolated. If selfishness is immaturity, and I believe that it is, there are certainly extenuating circumstances for that unripeness. For most of the years of our growth, we are conditioned and habituated to self-absorption. The baby plays with his toes, the child demands his toys, the adolescent seeks self-assurance. No doubt there are loving and giving moments in the life of the child or the youth, but the major work of an emerging ego is to build itself. It cannot yet afford the luxury and the generosity of true altruism.

Selfishness is a mark of immaturity because it indicates that the bearer of the mark has still a great deal of unfinished business that he never quite solved with his childish demands and his adolescent needs. He has no surplus to offer the world. Even religion at times is infected with this immaturity when it makes the worshiper concerned about *his* salvation, *his* personal redemption. If Freud and his successors are right—that maturity is evidenced by object-interest, the absorption in the welfare of another—how should we characterize many forms of religion which revolve around guarantees of individual and personal salvation? Must they not be judged and condemned by the highest standards as unripe, immature?

"Object-interest"—what a fruitful criterion of maturity this turns out to be! How illuminating it is to look at some contemporary philosophies with this lantern! Existentialism is devoted to the proposition that man begins with himself alone and, according to some of its prophets, he ends there also. Heidegger spoke of "the complete isolation of the free man, terribly alone with his own mortality. . . . From my loneliness in the face of death no one can save me. The free man is he who treats other people always as means, never as ends. When people are together, that togetherness is fraudulent—unauthentic: In the true world, there is room for only one solitary soliloquizing actor; others are just stage properties." This is Heidegger as described by Marjorie Grene in *Dreadful Freedom*. Does not this sound like the morbid self-centeredness of the adolescent, and the tortured adolescent at that? In this philosopher there is no room for an "object-interest." That is his disease: that he has not really advanced beyond the stage of the baby playing with his toes, the child hugging his toys to his bosom, fighting off all threats to his possessions, crying and whining about the coming of sleep and the loneliness of the night. It is interesting—is it not?—to see how a philosopher can artistically disguise these primitive immaturities, manifested in the incapacity to give love and concern to others, and to transform them into a creed of despair and aloneness. The child wants to be king—a sole sovereign; the child hates the dark; the child becomes philosopher and makes himself into a king by denying any relationship to others; he becomes monarch of all his self-made island, hypnotized and frozen by that ultimate dark room called death.

Sartre does not go to this extreme of poetic solipsism; he maintains that there is a relationship between one's self and other people. It is, however, one of conflict. Although it sounds absurd, Sartre maintains that one man becomes aware of another through feelings of fear and shame. A person is looked at or observed by a fellow human being and at that moment is threatened. The relationship between people, according to Sartre, is one of struggle, not of love; it is the attempt to make a thing out of somebody else before he can make a thing out of *me*. The war in life is between people who rush to take prisoners in order to avoid being taken as prisoners. There is certainly little sense of love or mutuality or shared values or gentle solicitude either in Heidegger or in Sartre. There is rather a sophisticated loneliness; the true iron curtain is between one person and another. If it is pierced or broken, it is only in order to take some captives, to serve as slaves in the dark mines of *my* will and *my* needs.

To view life as an inescapable relationship of conflict, to maintain that we human beings are bound together only by sadism and masochism, as torturer and being tortured, is to paint the world in perverse and even paranoiac colors. But what is more important in this connection is to point out that Sartre is self-revealed as an adolescent. Conflict is the very substance of adolescence. The youth is the one who feels insecure, threatened. How often does the stripling attack his parents or his family as a "preventive war"! Heidegger and Sartre are superb examples of immaturity, when it is defined as the lack of genuine "object-interest." The former is concerned only with himself and quite openly maintains that all other people are merely means to his end, instruments for his gratification. He says that that is true for all of life that applies to all human beings. But it is the child in Heidegger who has never been outgrown—the child who actually does use other people as means to his ends: as the source of milk, clothing, shelter, protection. The latter, Sartre, is not the child but rather the adolescent in the form of his thinking. He sees other people as threat, as menace, as attacker or as the object of his aggression, the target of his violence. This certainly is the mood of the confused, frightened, uncertain boy entering adolescence.

218

What the psychoanalysts call "object-interest" is termed "the dialogic principle" by the great Jewish theologian and philosopher, Martin Buber. In his book *Between Man and Man,* Buber emphasized that the greatness of life is to be found in the possibility of a real dialogue—a covenant between men and also between man and God. Some lovers are really in love only with themselves and their own passions. Some parents think that they love their children but really are concerned only with their own private matters. They are, as Buber said "manifold monologists with their mirrors."

True love comes when we want to be answerable for the other person "as one who is entrusted to me. . . . I wish his otherness to exist because I wish his particular being to exist."

To affirm another person, to be interested in his interests, to desire his fulfillment although it is different from your own—that is maturity. Today there is little of it because we feel so homeless, because our secure harbors of self-confidence have been blasted away by all the changes of our century. Man is today what Nietzsche said he was, "A problematic being . . . something dark and veiled . . . the animal that is not yet established." Man is sick because he is so ambiguous and because life is so ambiguous. That is why there is such an emphasis upon human solitude. A few centuries ago, men were certain of their status as children of God. Then came all of the discoveries of science, the unfolding of vast space and the dwarfing of our little earth into a minor star. We lost our cosmic security and are now more and more losing our sociological security. People have lost faith in democracy, in socialism, in communism, in all experiments. The modern world feels desperate at times, like a patient who has exhausted all doctors and all remedies. As long as there is a new and an untried specialist with some new medicine to offer, the patient retains hope; and then, when all alternatives have been tested and found wanting, nihilism sets in. Man today is like that patient; he has gone from faith to faith, from ideology and to ideology; he places his trust in science and religion, in nationalism, in Marxism; sometimes he has progressively tried all these proffered medicines and the tests seemed negative and the results almost nil. That is the source of much hopelessness and aloneness.

Buber understood this. He said, "Man finds himself alone with a universe which has become alien and uncanny. . . . Man reaches a condition when he can no longer stretch his hands out from his solitude, to meet a Divine form. . . . That is at the basis of Nietzsche's saying, 'God is dead'. . . . Apparently nothing more remains now for the solitary man but to seek an intimate communication with himself." This is what Heidegger does. Heidegger's "existence" is monological. When the man who has become solitary can no longer say "Thou" to the "dead" known God, everything depends on whether he can still say it to the living unknown God by saying "thou" with all his being to another living and known man. If he can no longer do this either, then there certainly remains for him the supreme illusion of detached thought, the thought that he is a self-contained self; as man, he is lost.

Buber brilliantly reveals the weakness of existentialism: "Life is not lived by my playing the enigmatic game on a board by myself. . . . Original guilt consists in remaining with one's self." The life of the solitary man is "the experience of a nightmare."

It appears to me, certainly, that much of modern life does have a nightmare quality about it. We feel pursued, appear naked and are threatened by giants—the giants of economic security and international war. Men who have lost a living belief in

God and for whom life has made it impossible to say "Thou" to other people and who have, therefore, lost faith in man likewise, such human beings are indeed lost in a grim nightmare, ready for sadism or suicide. The great question is how can we be awakened from this nightmare? Who will reassure us? Who will interpret our mad dreams as Joseph did Pharaoh's of old? Who can carry us from childish fear to mature courage?

The first necessity is to recognize that we do not begin life alone and that the frightened solitude of the existentialists is a cancer, a disease, a crippling defect. No matter how difficult the world may be or how threatening social reality may become, we can strive to achieve a mature "object-interest" in other people, throwing the bridge of love across the abyss of frustration. We can turn from the monologue to the dialogue, from aloneness to communion.

Where does a human being show the first signs of maturity? It is in the love that he gives to some independent person outside of his existence or to some ideal which is different from his own private wish or demand. A wise mother shows "object-interest" in devoting herself unquestioningly to the growth of her child— not according to her own needs but according to his. A man shows maturity in working with X-rays that lacerate his flesh but promise healing for the human race. The research scientist, the religious martyr, the man or woman who lives actually for the sake of truth, of beauty, or of goodness, sacrificing personal power or prestige in the quest of the larger good—such are the messengers of the kingdom of maturity. They have completed the revolution from parasite to patron, from taking child and fighting adolescent to giving adult. They know how to open the banks of their surplus and bless loved ones and humanity with the lavishness of their care.

Closely allied with this first test of maturity is the achievement of a larger self. We begin life narrowly imprisoned within our little bodies. Some people, tragically, never get a parole from that first prison. They go through life carefully watching every physical change, petting and soothing their skins, filling their flesh and mistaking that for living. More fortunate people learn as they develop that the real self does not stop with the body; it extends as far as our minds and imaginations can carry us; it includes as much territory as our souls can embrace. Pity the adult infant whose life is bounded by his body and its vicissitudes. Salute the adult who through sympathy and imagination makes himself part of the culture and the dreams of the ages, a companion of life both in triumph and in failure.

Judaism, interestingly enough, has always taught the necessity of obtaining an enlarged self. You recall the constant emphasis on "Remember that ye were slaves in the land of Egypt," and the equally constant emphasis on the lives of the patriarchs. Our religion, through these memories, stretched the Jewish ego so that it should become broad and big enough to include the tears of oppressed slaves, the thoughts of majestic sages, the ideals of prophets and rabbis. Our faith sensitized the individual Jew to become an inhabitant of time and a citizen of space. Through the study of the Torah, the centuries rolled through his mind and he became a contemporary of giants. Through the insistence of Judaism that its followers should remember that they were once strangers, that they should treat the oppressed and the alien as brothers, that they should never separate themselves from the needy or from the hungry, they were made citizens of space; the whole world of men entered the heart of the educated Jew. Maturity is movement from self-absorption to self-giving. From the narrow little island of the ego to the horizon as wide as the universe, inclusive of all of man's experience, pain, failure and

222

hope, to work for the largest and most inclusive self is the labor of adulthood.

A third sign of maturity, after "object-interest" and wide identification, is the proper management of emotions. A baby expresses what it feels—without control. An adolescent often represses what he feels—uncertain of its control. An adult manages his emotions—confident of inner mastery.

Ofttimes we are afraid of our emotional life. We know that we have in us a good deal of undischarged anger, hostility, lust and passion. We did not get all the rage out of our systems in the early years of our lives. We know that much of it is stored up like dynamite, and therefore we walk uneasily in the dark room of our emotions. In human personality, anxiety often becomes the substitute for rage. You see people frightened, filled with phobias, trembling; more often than not they are really trembling with a rage of which they themselves may not be conscious.

Whenever you find a person overly anxious, you know that you are in the presence of either a childish or an adolescent character. Why? Because it is natural for a child to be anxious about its security and its supply of love; it is also natural for an adolescent to be deeply concerned about the possibility of his mastering himself and his world. The youth, uncertain about the power of the dynamite of his passions, angers and untested abilities, experiences something quite like the anxiety of the physicists before the first atom bomb was tested in New Mexico in 1945. A mature person, having made his experiments, should know how to control the inner energy of his life. He should have achieved both an inspection and a management of the ore and all of the fissionable material in the mind of his spirit.

There are legitimate reasons for anxiety in the world. Anxiety plays many roles and serves many purposes. If you are anxious and suffer, you may, in the first place, have appeased your conscience which is guilty for one reason or another. Anxiety, in the second place, is a shield against aggression toward others, although it actually is a form of aggression toward one's self. In the third place, anxiety is the drawbridge against warm interrelationships with other people. If you are eaten up with fear and you are visibly crawling with all kinds of serpents of dread, you have no time for other people and you become, in turn, a repellent object to others. Anxiety is a marvelous method of escaping involvement with humanity. Finally, anxiety is a childish type of reassurance. You trembled once when you were little and your fear was wiped away in the warm embrace of a mother's arms. Tremble, man, again in the hope that protecting arms will miraculously embrace you.

The most important thing to understand about anxiety is its substitute nature; so often it really is the fraudulent version, the subtle translation, of rage. This is all-important because today many religious teachers and some philosophers make an absolute virtue out of anxiety. That is what the existentialists do; that is what Niebuhr proclaims in *The Nature and Destiny of Man*. Such writers maintain that anxiety is the absolute bedrock upon which profound human nature is erected.

I deny this. I assert on the contrary that *Angst* and *Sorge*—anxiety and care—yes, and dread, too—are masqueraders behind which hide the more fundamental realities of human anger and hostility. The basic experiences of an infant are fulfillment and frustration. This is the real dualism at the beginning of life: milk and no milk. The baby cries; he does not tremble. He protests rather than shivers. Anxiety is a later arrival. The pattern is somewhat as follows: frustration, anger, punishment for the anger, anxiety. This pattern goes on throughout life.

How many times, when we are filled with rage and know that we have to conceal it, do we experience, a day or a week later, a mysterious feeling of fear, a sense of insecurity, a basic anxiety? I say that when we human beings experience aggression and hostility, which we have been conditioned by both parental punishment and religious prohibition to regard as sinful, we change these emotions into anxiety. That is an acceptable emotion. A person who is filled with fear may be unhappy, but he is not stamped as immoral. In our Western culture it is permissible to torment one's self; in fact, that kind of masochism is almost a virtue in the Lutheran and Calvinist traditions. But emotional hostility and aggression are sins—dangerous threats to order, punishable emotional crimes. You have to hide these feelings behind the façade of dread. Notice how Kierkegaard and Kafka, who seem to make a virtue out of dread and anxiety, lived all their lives filled with hate and rage, partly recognized and partly unrecognized. Both artists were bitterly hostile to their fathers, but dared to express that hatred only in very disguised forms.

A mature person looks behind anxiety, faces his anger and masters it—just as he faces and masters other emotions. He knows how to renounce passion and ambition where necessary; he also knows how to give love without expecting it in return; he does not live his emotional life on a *quid pro quo* basis. A mature society will be one in which each person can become aggressive in some moments without feeling terribly guilty and in which each person can accept his need to depend upon others as well as to dominate others without any inner burden of self-accusation.

Proper management of emotions is one of the insignia of maturity.

A fourth mark of maturity is the ability to retain self-confidence despite many onslaughts upon it. The child lacks self-confidence; so does the adolescent. The mature man with the proper humility nevertheless lives his life in calm awareness of his value and of his strength. He does not allow himself to become the victim of wounded self-esteem.

There are many subtle indications to this aspect of maturity. Life certainly inflicts many wounds upon our self-esteem. It batters us with pain; it can put us under the microscope of unimportance; it turns the ground of our work and love quite often into quicksand. This is when a character demonstrates its tensile strength or its tragic weakness.

The self-esteem necessary for achieving maturity can be deeply wounded even by certain religious doctrines, such as the concept of original sin and the need for the intervention of divine power to atone for it on behalf of mankind. In Judaism, according to rabbinic teaching, man himself plays a most decisive and responsible role in the cosmos. He himself can bring God near him in the world or remove him. His own deeds are of first importance in Judaism. Furthermore, God, portrayed as the Active Creator, has man as His partner; man imitates Him in deeds of active creation.

For many centuries Western religion stressed the dependence of man upon Divine Grace. Then with the coming of the Renaissance, man revolted against that dependence and during these last several centuries has been asserting himself. This overreaction, while it has brought some blessings in the form of democracy and individualism, has carried man to the outer edge of value-chaos. Today there is a beginning of the recognition of man as a creator in the context of a greater Creative Good. Where man is regarded by religion as important to God or as a co-worker with God, there his self-esteem is not wounded or destroyed: there he achieves the foundations of self-confidence in life and in the God of life.

One of the tragedies of today is that so many have ceased to believe either in Divine Love or in human love. If man has no heavenly Father, as Sartre maintains, and if all human relationships are tainted with conflict, as Sartre also maintains, then man certainly cannot have any self-esteem.

I find in Judaism a superb wisdom leading to maturity. The faith of Israel never wounded man's self-esteem, never castrated him, never made him a eunuch of the spirit, never sent him to the depths of impotence, but on the contrary, has always given man a sense of importance and a tremendous ethical and spiritual role to play.

Self-confidence, in spite of all of the onslaughts of life: this trait of maturity is found in its highest development in Jewish history and experience. It can be argued that the people of Israel should have lost confidence centuries ago. They should have regressed to infantilism, and become completely schizoid or paranoid. They had the vision which prevented them from perishing. Abraham had every reason in the world for losing self-confidence. He was tested again and again. He did not surrender. Job is another example of mature self-confidence. He continued to walk in the integrity of his ways. He did not either blame himself or accept blame for the tragedies that overcame him. When his friends came to preach to him about his sins as the cause of his suffering, he courageously repudiated that interpretation. Nor did he hesitate to list his own virtues, quietly and humbly but firmly manifesting a proper self-evaluation. Job was mature enough to approach his tragic situation with profoundly impersonal perspective, discovering the sources of frustration not in his deeds but rather in the mysterious nature of the universe and the indecipherable ways of God.

Another criterion of maturity appears in the way that we look upon ourselves and with what expectations we approach life. An individual who is filled with great expectations and restless unless he achieves all of them is still an adolescent. It means that he yet dwells in the fantasy realm. Religion, both Jewish and Christian, has always made a virtue of modesty. The humility both of Moses and of Jesus is portrayed with loving care in the literature of the spirit. May we not now add modesty about our human expectations to the list of psychological virtues? As one grows, one learns to temper and to modify his imperious demands. If he does not, then he is not only miserable but unripe. The child is ravishingly hungry for everything; his appetite for new experience often seems quite limitless. Similarly, the adolescent often is quite breathless in the pursuit of an infinite number of goals, many quite contradictory. He does not know what he wants; by trial and error, he becomes disciplined into an awareness of his limitations, a knowledge that he must choose between a multitude of ambitions. What is legitimate in childhood and youth is quite out of place in adulthood. The appetite for restless achievement has to be curbed, modified. I see frequently what happens when this control is lacking. Men and women try to gorge themselves on money, power, and prestige—and they somehow are still hungry.

Such men and women have never learned the art of proper dieting, they still gulp the foods of overdemanding expectations. There is sugar in the blood among the spiritual diabetics—those who eat unwisely at the table of ruthless self-demand. Or at times there is too much salt in the meal of maturity, leading to a malfunction of the arteries and the kidneys, the whole organism of the psyche. The salt of the drive for success, the sugar of the ceaseless striving for power, eaten with compulsive nervousness in our competitive society, bring spiritual and emotional death. A person becomes adult when he places himself upon a balanced diet of expectation and limitation, when he realizes that the metabolism of adulthood should be quite different from that of the earlier years of existence and the caloric intake far more limited than in the wild and growing years of the first two decades upon earth.

I do not mean to minimize the value of great ideals and large horizons. We should avoid apathy as well as agony. The success mania of a capitalistic society creates the danger of the latter—agony. Just because there seem to be not enough medals to go around, we have to learn that the medals themselves—the medals of power and prestige—are often really the badges of immaturity—medals won in races appropriate only to youth, but quite unbecoming the ripe character of maturity.

Perhaps Judaism in its great stress upon equality was subtly enunciating this truth; that we human beings should not torment ourselves with false competitiveness, with a mad rush for absolute and unattainable goals. The rabbis of Israel stressed not only modesty and humility, but also equality—the sovereign and equal value of every human personality whether humble craftsman or artisan or learned scholar and sage. The doctrine of equality so fundamental to Jewish teaching is not only an ethical principle but a psychological medicine—an antidote against psychic overexpectation and consequent deflation. It assures every human being of the importance and the value of his work in the world.

A mature person has conquered an earlier gluttony for absolute power, achievement, success; he has become more modest in his drafts upon the bank of life. Furthermore, he has learned that it is essential to select one dominant value out of the many possible values of life and to organize his character around that ruling interest or goal. He has transcended the inconsistency and daydreaming of the adolescent who vacillates from day to day. To the adult mind, the choice of one career, one mate, one religion, means that he has organized his existence about a central shrine. He does not run from idol to idol in pursuit of a will-o'-the-wisp. You can tell a mature person rather well by the harmony that exists within him between competing impulses all subordinated to the baton of the master conductor—the ruling principle of his life.

The analogy of a symphony orchestra is pertinent here. There are violins and cellos, woodwinds, brass, and percussion instruments in every one of us. Unless all are guided by the ruling hand of a conductor—the dominant attitude of creativity—musical chaos results in the concert hall of our souls. If, on the other hand, a stern but artistic maestro stands upon the podium—the ruling value of maturity—there will be harmony rather than eternal discord in the life symphony of a human being. He will have established a master hand, a dominant value, one ruling ideal and goal, as the wielder of the baton of inner beauty.

Now, I do not maintain that it is easy to achieve inner compatibility in this kind of world. Erich Fromm, in his book *Man for Himself,* brilliantly points out how many different roles a man has to play to achieve success. It is not only the "huckster" in the advertising world who must change his face and his voice a dozen times a day; everyone in our whole merchant-man society has to put on the mask of geniality and joviality, to force the hearty laugh and the bluff chuckle in order to "make a deal" or "please the customer" or attain "a winning personality." Capitalism places an enormous strain upon men and women, making them play incompatible games within themselves; they are afraid to be natural, to express their genuine moods, to articulate their honest ambitions and desires.

Much of our unhappiness today comes from the fact that men and women nervously have to put off and take on many costumes in the course of a day, costumes of pretense about their feelings and their work. While we may not be able to solve this enormous problem for society as a whole, each of us can begin with himself and determine to develop true integrity within the framework and limitations of economic necessity. We can begin, at least, the process of inner consistency, of finding a pattern of life which will satisfy our major drives for beauty or usefulness or helpfulness or love.

I mentioned before the existence of many moods as well as of many roles in every person. Sometimes we really do demand too much of ourselves and expect ourselves to achieve a perfect consistency and compatibility. This, too, is wrong. Emotional maturity is never absolute but only relative. There are elements of childish insecurity and adolescent aggressiveness in every one of us. The thing to avoid is going over the boundary line to too great a quantity of childishness or aggression. All that we should expect is that our mature moods should predominate in the symphony of our existence.

To conquer one's self means to organize one's self, to equip one's self with a proper hierarchy of inner values. In Jewish history we know that our sages disciplined themselves to set certain goals as the central shrines of personality. They not only stressed worship of God and work for the triumph of His moral will, but also made learning the dominant trait of Jewish existence. Learning was for them a form of nonviolent competition in contrast to war or power-seeking—forms of adolescent racing and rivalry. The study of the Torah, the dominant motif in the symphony of Jewish life, was a mature organizing principle for Jewish sanity. The religion of Israel in other ages arranged for the fulfillment of two basic needs of man: submission and dominance—submission to the will of God on the one hand, and on the other, dominance through personal achievement in scholarship, a nondestructive, indeed a spiritually productive, attribute of the wise life.

There are many other marks of maturity which might be mentioned: an acceptance of reality rather than of the pleasure principle as a guide to conduct; the willingness to fight rather than to flee in the presence of danger; the achievement of a truly parental and giving attitude toward the world. These, however, are implicit in many of the other criteria of maturity on which we have elaborated.

Our analysis so far has led us, it is to be hoped, to a deeper appreciation of maturity and immaturity. In the light of this analysis, how immature our modern culture really is! Pessimism, for example, is not only a reaction to real danger; it is often a "flight manifestation." You find the world is difficult; therefore you flee into defeatism and negation. This is quite reminiscent of the child who fails to get his way and so throws a tantrum, or of the adolescent who sulks in his tent of aloneness or frustration. How many poets and writers of our time manifest the further immaturity of abysmal self-pity! Their immaturity may be subtly disguised as concern for man or as sadness about the state of the world. Penetrate beneath the disguise, however, and you will find a child feeling sorry for himself.

Earlier, we defined maturity as "object-interest." The child in its self-absorption, we said, has little real "object-interest." He is compelled to use his parents as the means for the satisfaction of his needs. Here is the origin of the "exploitative" type of man, whom Fromm identifies and describes. Competitive capitalism in this sense, encourages the childish in us by making us look upon other people as servants of our wishes or workers for our private profit. The adolescent, also, with his competitiveness really has little loving "object-interest." He sees "the other" as a rival or as a threat. It is only when we become truly adult that we can become interested in other people with solicitude for their welfare, a giving of love without demand of immediate return.

In religion we find these three types quite prominent—the child type of worshiper who tries to make of God the eternal Giver without any reciprocity upon the part of the communicant; the adolescent who turns against God or rebels against Him, whose religion becomes a matter of strife and conflict; and the adult type beyond infantile dependence and adolescent competitiveness who has achieved a true "object-interest" in God's world and its abiding values.

It may be interesting to look at Judaism in terms of this psychological analysis of maturity and immaturity. Judaism has certainly always emphasized "fight philosophy"—a struggle against the evils of life and the injustices of the world, rather than an ascetic withdrawal or flight into private purity or monastic aloneness. It has called upon man to be a participant in the struggle and not a mere spectator who remains on the sidelines of life.

The stress placed in the Jewish religion upon the future, upon the flexible process of Becoming, upon striving and working for a better world for tomorrow, mirrors maturity. The truly adult character is able to live for the future because he is not morbidly preoccupied with his childish or adolescent past. Neurotics are always enslaved to the Egypts of their own past; psychic freedom really means liberation from the scarring wounds of babyhood or youth.

When we turn to the Bible, we can certainly find many marvelous hints of maturity in the characters and events of that immortal work. The story of Adam and Eve, for example, is the saga of the birth of conscience; it is also the proclamation of the reality principle that mankind inevitably has to move from the Garden of Eden of his childhood to the sweat of adult frustration and fulfillment.

The stories of Cain and Abel, Jacob and Esau, both supply dramatic examples of the eternal sibling rivalry, the never-ending competitiveness between children of the same family. Abraham is the prototype of profound maturity, the man who proclaimed to life his faith in it "in spite of everything," that is, in spite of every trial and every sorrow. It is he also who, in his plea for the wicked cities of Sodom and Gomorrah, searches for even a small minority of righteous men as armor against destruction, and so indicates to us that we too should always seek in ourselves for at least some evidence of creative and righteous moods and acts, even in times of inner betrayal or failure.

Jacob's "limping upon his thigh" is the immortal reminder of the truth that life inflicts its wounds upon everyone. Joseph carries us from spoiled childhood to mature adulthood. He who sought everything from his father and who tried to take everything away from his brothers became at last the giver and the provider in times of famine. Moses portrays the necessity of law in life, of the acceptance of discipline, the ability to take hostility and ingratitude without breaking; his is the voice summoning the people to go forward into the unknown, which is the supreme test of mature courage. The prophets of Israel are valiant heroes enunciating the immortal philosophy of "fight and not flight"— to use the formula of Leon Saul: Amos and Jeremiah were not spectators but participants in the magnificent battle against un-

righteousness and injustice. Jonah exemplifies the Jewish motif
—that there is always hope, that man is not condemned to the
prison of fixity, that this is an open world and that true repentance and creative reconstruction of the inner life can avert doom,
even as the inhabitants of Ninevah by repentance in a new life
turned aside the decree of destruction. Job is in his way the example of maturity—a man who has proper self-love and self-
respect, a soul walking in the integrity of his ways in spite of
tragedy and suffering.

Immaturity is a danger not only for personal happiness but for
social survival as well. Arthur Koestler insists that authoritarian
systems like fascism and communism have a far greater appeal
for the mass of men than democracy. If this be true, then it is an
index to the stunted development of twentieth-century man. Dictatorship attracts men only because it promises to satisfy the
dependency needs of the child within us.

Are individual and social immaturity inescapable, then? Have
we no hope? Or if we do have hope, what facts are on the side
of human growth and human progress? Furthermore, what shall
we do with ourselves and our children in order to escape pro-
longed immaturity?

As we live, we should learn to evaluate ourselves rather im-
personally. We should stop every once in a while and ask,
"What am I doing? How am I acting? Am I reasonably consistent or do I blow hot and cold every few days? Do I look upon
life as a cup out of which I may give sweet wine to others, or do
I greedily hug the chalice of selfishness to my own bosom? Are
there no drops for the parched lips of others?" We ought to take
stock from time to time, and if we find ourselves living life pretty
much as a monologue, if we are filled with self-pity, are thin-
skinned and easily wounded in our feelings, unsmiling in our

rigid demands for protection or success, quick to take offense, speedy to hurt and be hurt, walking around and around in the prison of self-interest, then we will know that we are still frightened children or bewildered adolescents.

Every one of us requires a new freedom—a liberation from frozen attitudes and fixed expectations. We need latitude and longitude in our development from dependence to independence. We need to be able to express anger, love, fear, anxiety, all without too heavy a burden of guilt.

Furthermore, we require a great tolerance for ourselves and for others. As we mature in school, we come to learn many vagaries of grammar in language. Why should we not become emotionally prepared for the vagaries in human behavior? "In the beginning is vagary"—this is the law of human life. True, we can come to conjugate many a verb and to parse many a sentence, but the language of life remains always inevitably idiomatic, and we come across the unexpected continually in ourselves and in our dear ones. "Expect the unexpected" is a rather safe law for preserving sanity.

Or let me put it in another way. In every phase of human development we enter a new country, as it were, and therefore have to try to learn a new language. Some people always speak a broken dialect; they never can get used to the novel demands of adolescence or adulthood. When we come to puberty or, in fact, to any crisis period, we are like strangers disembarking on foreign soil. We need Baedekers and conversation manuals to make us feel at home in this new territory.

Nor is the scenery monotonous in the inner country of man. There are jungles and valleys and mountain peaks: love, aggression, sexuality, possessiveness. Anyone who expects the landscape of emotion to be simple is headed for great disillusionment. The inner landscape is always reminiscent of the six days of Creation, where multitudes of new forms appeared upon the earth. And yet, for all of the variety, God could say, "It is good." We ought to learn how to imitate God in this sense: to affirm the goodness of the manifoldness in ourselves and in others. One way to achieve maturity is to recognize that there is something wild as well as something orderly in our makeup; the art of life is to domesticate and to tame and to sublimate the wild and the tempestuous elements within our inner landscape, to make the barren soil bring forth sweet fruits.

Nor is this impossible. The hope for maturity lies in the fact that some among the sages and the saints of mankind have indeed mastered the childish and the adolescent, have outgrown the mad search for power and are "pilot plants" proving that mass production of goodness is attainable. We are told today by pessimists or cynics that men prefer immaturity or childishness and that that is why dictatorship is the wave of the future. I disagree completely with this point of view. The great hope of life consists in the very fact that normal men and women have within them an urge to mature and a drive to grow up; when they do regress to childishness and dependency, they do so with terrible wounds to their pride and their self-esteem. There is the yearning to become adult. Social science today and tomorrow should show the leaders of a democracy how to play effectively upon the desires of men and women for adulthood, to bring them into the open and to make people conscious of how really ashamed they are of their flight from responsibility into the arms of any totalitarian government.

I say that democracy will win because people cannot psychologically remain satisfied with infantilism or adolescence. There is hope for maturity just because more and more human beings are becoming aware of their unhappiness when they stop too long at the childish or the youthful stages of evolution. A great deal of anxiety, fear and guilt will vanish when psychological wisdom will teach all of us that we have to grow up—become free and independent—or pay the price of lifelong misery and confusion. The very biological and emotional forces in us drive us along the road toward adulthood—the kind of adulthood which is neither afraid of legitimate dependence on other people at moments nor aggressively assertive of one's own powerful and isolated self-sufficiency.

Biology and psychology as well as religion assure us that maturity is both possible and ultimately inevitable for the human race. We sometimes can get bogged down in the mud of frustration; and other times we make many foolish detours, but the road and the direction are there; and we in the twentieth century can begin traveling along that highway of hope. I say this in spite of violence and the threat of war and all of the tragedies of suffering people.

Life awakens us to a strange world of sounds and colors, of milk and laughter, of tears and love. It prods us to walk like a reluctant schoolboy along the road to youth and maturity. Then, the twilight creeps over the horizon. Age takes possession of the house of the body and the court of the mind. If we are wise, we can greet age with serenity, without disenchantment or bitterness. The philosopher George Santayana in his eighty-sixth year published a beautiful essay quite pertinent to my thought. He said, "Life is an opportunity or occasion for good and evil alike and death is an insurance against both . . . Old age, death and silence are not by any means in my opinion evil in themselves . . . Why should I say of good things that the fact that they have an end infects their existence with evil? . . .

Nothing can spoil them while they exist except failure to fulfill their natural functions . . . It is limping life and corrupt youth that infect their excellence . . ."

Santayana, in other words, in his old age believed that life at each stage of existence has its own beauty and its own fulfillment. We should always seek to avoid ugliness and corruption. Old age and death in their time are to be accepted with the same natural piety as are the glowing sun and the radiant light of youth. We can look forward to many portraits of life being painted by the wiser generations yet to come.

CHAPTER NINE

Is Life Worth Living Today?

FIVE ROADS TO EMOTIONAL MATURITY

"Is life worth living today?" is an emotional question and not an intellectual one. We are in the realm of our most intimate personal feelings when we ask this question, and our task is to make our feelings as mature as our bodies are mature.

Many of us are just beginning to understand that there are at least three different kinds of maturity: physical, intellectual and emotional. Because we are all subject to sense impressions, we often suffer from the illusion that a man or woman who is grown up in body and adult in mind must necessarily be mature in feelings. Nothing could be further from the truth. A person may be an intellectual giant and an emotional dwarf at one and the same time. It is this disparity which makes life so difficult. Now we are just at the beginning of discovering a curriculum and a discipline for emotional maturity. Man probably roamed the surface of the earth for countless aeons, physically mature but intellectually and emotionally infantile. Then came the growth of language, the discovery of writing and other arts of communication, the birth of science. From the time of Plato to John Dewey, the emphasis on education has been primarily upon the acquisition of knowledge, training in skills, and victory over nature. We have learned how to develop strong muscles and clever minds. We are just now beginning to realize the necessity to develop mature emotions. What gymnastics has done for the body, mathematics for the mind, an emerging psychology may yet do for the soul of man. Humanity will never be happy, the world will never be at peace, life will never be truly worth living, until we have become artists of emotional adjustment and until we have learned to manage ourselves as well as our bodies, nature and matter.

There are, it seems to me, five roads to emotional maturity. The first is to be brave enough to accept our own imperfections. This was one of Alfred Adler's most brilliant insights; he called this the courage of imperfection. Somewhere in our childhood we develop exaggerated notions of what we want to be and of what life demands of us. Some of us never escape that compulsion to achieve perfection. Because in adult life we find incompleteness everywhere, we feel a civil war raging between what we once dreamed of being and what we must necessarily become. How many there are who go throughout life eaten away by a sense of inadequacy and of inferiority, living under the unneccessary tension of trying to be better and abler and more successful than their fellows. As Dr. Rollo May points out, "the so-called faultless painter of the Renaissance, Andrea del Sarto, was decidedly second-rate; the giant of them all, Michelangelo, himself realized how far short he fell of perfection." Genuine success, measured by the ultimate contribution to humanity, requires that one accept imperfection in one's field of endeavor.

Nature does not demand that we be perfect. It requires only that we grow. In work, in art, in friendship, in love, we are all amateurs. Unhappiness can come from the fact that we too often take the all-or-nothing attitude toward the universe. Life is not a matter of "all" or "none"; it is "more" or "less." All of us are handicapped in one way or another; all of us are destined to experience suffering and disillusionment. All of us are going to shed many tears and shout with much laughter before our day is finished. Oliver Wendell Holmes once said that his greatest feeling of relief came when he realized that he was not called upon to be God, that man is never called upon to be God. We are frail children of dust, imperfect, striving toward perfection, but fortunately never achieving that static, unmoving goal.

We go through many stages in our development. As children and as youths we often come to expect life to give us unblemished joy, unstained happiness. Sometimes we share the ecstatic optimism of a Browning or a Walt Whitman and declare that the whole earth is good and it is sheer joy to be alive. Then pain intrudes upon our paradise and we become disillusioned and give way to despair. "Life," we say, "is imperfect; friends are deceitful, fame is fleeting, love is fickle." The way to a mature happiness is to move from the stage when we say "yes" to all of life, through that stage when we say "no" to all of life, and then on to the ultimate stage when we say "in spite of." In spite of disappointment, sorrow, frustration, imperfection, we can make life worth living, friendship worth treasuring, love worth serving, work worth doing. This is the true human situation. Man, becoming healthy, learns to affirm himself even though he is imperfect and also to affirm his fellow men. We come to love others because of their faults as well as their virtues. They are human like ourselves. They are our fellow men. This perhaps is the ultimate meaning of the phrase "Thou shalt love they neighbor as thyself." We begin to take ourselves and our neighbors for what all of us are.

The courage of imperfection means, therefore, that while we

shall strive always to achieve the best in our power, we shall not torment ourselves continually by seeking to make an absolute out of our relative achievements. Many human beings go throughout life punishing themselves more severely than anyone else could possibly punish them, criticizing themselves, inwardly tearing themselves down, disparaging their own worth. Such self-flagellation shows that the individual has not grown up, that he has not become able to face himself and his conflicts and his impulses without too much disturbance about them. Creative growth should be the goal. When we accept this truth, we learn that failure and error are ofttimes as valuable teachers as success and achievement. We are not put here on earth to become rivals of God. We do not carry, like Atlas, the weight of the world. We are to be struggling, aspiring human beings, aware always of the fact that there is a chasm between what we are and what we ought to be, but never permitting that chasm to become the source of our destruction, the grave of our happy adjustment to life. Long ago the rabbis whose ideas are presented in *Perke Aboth* (*The Sayings of the Fathers*) understood this great psychological truth. Rabbi Tarfon said, "The work is not upon thee to finish, nor art thou free to desist from it."

The second way to make life worth living is to develop a mature conscience. Life often becomes a burden because we are afflicted with an overwhelming sense of guilt and of sin. The psychologist's distinction between a grown-up conscience and a childhood conscience is still quite unknown to most people. A childish conscience is built out of the inevitable frustrations of the childhood periods, because many things have to be forbidden a child which are perfectly manageable and permissible in adult life. Yet multitudes of people carry with them through adult life the infantile conscience of childhood. Life often seems

not worth living to men because they see the accusing finger
wherever they turn; they hear the reverberating echo of "It's
wrong" resounding ceaselessly in their minds. I remember seeing
many years ago a motion picture called *The Way of All Flesh*. I
remember the impression that Emil Jannings made upon me as
he walked through the streets of the city feeling that he had
committed an unforgivable crime: before his terrified eyes all
the electric signs seemed to read "Murderer! Thief!"

Life becomes a burden to many men and women because they
too go through the streets of experience feeling that upon the
signposts of life are written the words "Failure! Deceiver! Hyp-
ocrite! Sensualist!" Certainly men do sometimes commit crimes
against their loved ones and against human society on an adult
level, crimes which are real sins and which do require real
atonement, reparation, repentance. How much of human life, on
the other hand, is now made miserable because men carry childhood prohibitions into adult life where they no longer have any
real justification. When we are infants, our fathers and mothers
have to protect us against falling, have to erect barriers against
our stumbling feet, force distasteful medicine down our unwilling throats. For our own growth we are not permitted
freedom, self-reliance, independence. Lacking judgment and
experience, we are impressed with many "Thou shalt nots"
which serve to guide and protect our growing muscles and our
expanding spirits. The tragedy often is that the protecting barriers of childhood become the encasing prison doors of maturity,
that the necessary prohibitions of our infancy become the destructive inhibitions of our maturity, that dependent reliance
upon others becomes indecisiveness, inappropriate to the grown-
up world. We become afraid to liberate ourselves from the
chains of yesteryear. We are afraid to trust our mature judgment

and to realize that we now have within us the capacity to distinguish between right and wrong, good and evil, cruelty and kindness, and that we can trust our mature consciences to guide us aright through difficult temptations. It is only when we become liberated from the haunting voices of decades ago, only when we become liberated from the prohibitions and commandments which served our childhood needs but which are tragically out of place in adulthood—it is only then that we can become free, healthy personalities, making life worth the struggle.

The third way to make life worth living is to develop courage, the kind of courage that gives us a combative spirit. Just as it is not usual for a religious leader to say that there is a danger of overworking the conscience, so it is not usual for him to praise the combative spirit. Yet, there is a danger in too much sweetness and light. Life becomes depressing when we falsify ourselves, when we try to distort the realities of our experience and pretend that we are something that we are not. No human being is born into this world an angel. We are creatures who come with anger, hostility, and pugnacity as primal instincts of our natural endowment. We are assured by the physiologists that aggressiveness even has its own special physical organs, the adrenal glands, and that if these do not function normally a man cannot have any kind of character that is vigorously worthwhile. Like the rest of our primitive instincts, combativeness can be grievously misused, but like the rest of them also, it is an indispensable ingredient of human vigor not to be eliminated but to be sublimated and put to creative uses. Winston Churchill may be taken as a symbol of the combative spirit of the man who knows how to become angry and use that anger for great constructive ends. Paul Ehrlich made in his laboratory six hundred five attempts before he found the formula for the cure for a dread disease. He knew how to use courage and combativeness. We have to learn how to be active and aggressive in life. No worthwhile thing is ever accomplished without the harnessing of these magnificent servants of human energy to a great purpose.

The trouble is that here, too, we are misled by our childhood experiences. When we were very young, we had undirected temper spasms, anger tantrums. We were punished and we learned that we must control our hostility, that to give expression to it leads to punishment or what is even worse, threats of punishment. So many human beings grow up into excessively timid personalities who are afraid of their own shadows and so keep their antipathies to themselves. Since they cannot express a normal quantity of anger against the outer world, they turn upon the safest object of their wrath, namely, themselves, and make themselves miserable and their loved ones miserable and their lives often an overpowering burden. Many unhappy people have to learn the art of being constructively pugnacious; he who never expresses his hostility against things outside himself will be nonetheless giving vent to it within himself. The fear of expressing oneself against others results in the destruction of one's own self. We are imperfect human beings. Anger is one of the expressions of our imperfection. The scientist working vigorously against the evils of nature is one example of the way that we can express our innermost feelings and harness our combativeness to great redemptive causes. If we want to make life worth living, we too need to express a normal amount of aggressiveness insofar as life itself permits. Instead of its being a withering destructive force, however, aggressiveness can be channeled into a creative attack upon disease, injustice, slum districts, delinquency, war—all the manifold evils which can give us the moral equivalent of hatred.

The fourth way to make life worth living is to adopt a long-range scale of values. As we grow up, we have to give up certain momentary pleasures for the sake of more lasting pleasures. Every level of our development requires that we deny ourselves for the sake of more lasting satisfactions. This does not mean that we should not have our moments of ease, of relaxation, of unburdened leisure, but it does mean that we must be able to measure the temporary pleasures of the moment against the permanent joys of a lifetime. The more immature we are, the more we cry out for the satisfaction of inconsistent and irreconcilable delights. The more mature we become, the more we realize that what Plato said was true: that we have to become experts in using the scale of measurement. We have to weigh a present pain against a future pleasure and a present pleasure against a future pain. To do this well is to become an artist in the values of life.

Not only in our personal lives, but also in the life of humanity we must have the ability to live in long-term values instead of short-time values. We should know that the defeat of the moment is not the defeat of eternity, that civilization is a tougher plant than we usually imagine. It has its roots widely scattered over the surface of the earth, and even when the drought of war comes as a blight to wither some of its tendrils, nevertheless it sends forth bud and blossom and rich fruit in other climates and in other times. We who live through an age of fire and hail and snow are often too much overwhelmed to feel the coming of new life beneath our feet and the promise of a new day concealed beyond the fogged horizon. Life will not perish with us; humanity will not die when we die. Culture will not disappear with our generation or our century. We can live only with the resolve to make our best contribution to whatever culture shall survive and to live for the triumph of men whom we shall never know, in ages that we shall never experience. This also is maturity—spiritual maturity. Even as we are the heirs of martyrs, saints and heroes who lived and died for us and in their death gave birth to our world of conflict, so are we the ancestors of an unpredictable, creative, demanding human society yet in the womb of time.

The fifth way to make life worth living is the way of love. This sounds like a simple prescription. It is perhaps the most difficult of all tasks. We are told that the word "love" should be used in the broad sense of true friendliness with other human beings, of one's considering the interests of other individuals as well as oneself. Probably the most important cause of unhappiness is the incapacity to give affection and love to others. This is the predicament of the egocentric; it leads to failure, to illness and despair.

We are all acquainted with the story of Narcissus, who fell in love with his own image in the water. In extreme cases of insanity, people sometimes lose all interest in the outside world; life for them goes on only within a self-created vacuum. Yet there are infinite numbers of so-called normal people who are narcissists, who are interested only in self-aggrandizement, who can see in other people only an audience that can give admiration, praise, and affection. The result is loneliness and unhappiness. It is futile to tell such people that they are selfish, that they are egotistical, that they are immoral. Their self-love is merely a symptom of insecurity and fear, which comes from early childhood experience. When the little boy feels that he is rejected, when he feels that there is a lack of love for him from those most important in his life, he may turn all of his own capacity for affection onto himself. He is forced into the position of loving himself as he would want his parents to love him. This is one of the reasons that marital unhappiness and divorce bring so much danger to the growing children who need love and understanding as they will never need it again.

Egocentricity is perhaps the most tragic of all the causes of cynicism and pessimism. An individual may be so deeply concerned with his own self that he believes that he constructs his own universe, establishes his own truth or falsehood and writes his own Ten Commandments. Such an individual tends to become swamped in his own subjectivity.

"Man who bows down to nothing," said Dostoevski, "can never bear the burden of himself." Ibsen, in his remarkable description of a lunatic asylum in *Peer Gynt*, showed that he understood this matter thoroughly: "Each one is shut up within the cask of himself. . . . None has a tear for others' woes or cares what any other thinks. . . . Long live the emperor of Self!" Being excessively self-centered is a symptom of mental illness. People who suffer from extreme sensitiveness, from a persecution complex, from fear of their neighbors and of the opinions of others, all make the mistake of assuming that everyone is concerned with them. They define the universe in terms of their own little egos.

To avoid this tragic fate we have to feel that there are persons and causes and powers outside our own egos worthy of our devotion, our loyalty, and our love. The more we avoid narcissism, the truer become our cooperative attitude, our sense of interdependence and of our mutual growth with others, the happier becomes our own personal destiny and the richer our own individual joy. This is the paradox about the world: that he who wishes to find himself must lose himself. Hillel said that "He who aggrandizes his name loses his name."

We shall never find life worth living so long as we remain

imprisoned within our own little egos. The secret of survival and success in the world is to place one's ego at the service of loved ones, of large social purposes, of great causes.

The world of tomorrow is going to need more healthy-minded, well-adjusted, sane spirits than ever before. If we keep these five ways of emotional maturity steadily before us, we shall be able to affirm that life is worth the struggle. It is worth it in its own terms and because it gives us the possibility of making those terms better for the infinite generations yet to come. Suffering we shall certainly undergo, failures we shall certainly encounter, tragedy will often be our lot. Yet we can create an unconquerable human spirit that proclaims, in spite of all and through it all, that "life can be made worth living."

There *is* hope for man.

About the Author

DR. JOSHUA LOTH LIEBMAN *was not only rabbi of Temple Israel, Boston, but one of the leading radio preachers in America. His sermons over NBC, ABC and CBS coast-to-coast networks and his regular Sunday broadcasts to the six New England states had listeners numbering in the millions.*

During the last few years of his life, Dr. Liebman served as university preacher at Harvard, Cornell, Vassar, Dartmouth, Wellesley, Smith, and other leading colleges and universities. He was Visiting Professor of Jewish Philosophy and Literature at the Boston University School of Theology and at Andover-Newton Theological Seminary; and it is believed that he was the first rabbi invited to become a regular member of a Christian theological seminary to teach Judaism to Christian clergymen.

Dr. Liebman studied at the Hebrew University in Jerusalem and the Hebrew Union College in Cincinnati, where he took his doctorate in Jewish philosophy. He was a member of the Governor's Committee on Racial and Religious Understanding for Massachusetts, and was the chairman of the Governor's Committee of Clergymen. During World War II he served as a mem-

ber of the *Committee on Army and Navy Religious Activities,* directing the work of Jewish chaplains.

In 1946, when he was just thirty-nine, Dr. Liebman's *Peace of Mind* was published and immediately sprang to the head of the best-seller lists. Twenty years later, the original edition is in its fortieth printing and over 900,000 copies have been sold, while millions more have appeared in paperback form and in nine foreign languages.

His death in 1948 was felt as a personal loss by the countless numbers whose lives he had entered through his teachings.